SAMURAI
RISING

SAMURAI

The Epic Life of Minamoto Yoshitsune

RISING

Pamela S. Turner
Illustrated by Gareth Hinds

 Charlesbridge TEEN

For Connor Townsend and my friends at Berkeley Kendo Dojo and Oakland Kendo Dojo—P. S. T.

For Sara Norton and Jim Kelso, who helped a nerdy, head-strong boy explore Japanese culture; and to Bill Gleason Sensei, who brought me back to aikido—G. H.

First paperback edition 2018
Text copyright © 2016 by Pamela S. Turner
Illustrations copyright © 2016 by Gareth Hinds
Page 27: "This forgotten tree . . . turns to sorrow": From The Tale of the Heike, translated by Royall Tyler, translation copyright © 2012 by Royall Tyler. Used by permission of Viking Books, an imprint of Penguin Publishing Group, a division of Penguin Random House LLC.
Page 163: "A dream of warriors . . . summer grasses": Classical Japanese Prose: An Anthology compiled and edited by Helen Craig McCullough, copyright © 1990 by the Board of Trustees of the Leland Stanford Jr. University. All rights reserved. Used with the permission of Stanford University Press, www.sup.org.

Published by Charlesbridge
9 Galen Street
Watertown, MA 02472
(617) 926-0329
www.charlesbridgeteen.com

Library of Congress Cataloging-in-Publication Data
Turner, Pamela S.
    Samurai rising: the epic life of Minamoto Yoshitsune/Pamela S. Turner; with illustrations by Gareth Hinds.
        pages cm
    ISBN 978-1-58089-584-2 (reinforced for library use)
    ISBN 978-1-58089-585-9 (softcover)
    ISBN 978-1-60734-848-1 (ebook)
    ISBN 978-1-60734-849-8 (ebook pdf)
    1. Minamoto, Yoshitsune, 1159–1189—Juvenile literature. 2. Generals—Japan—Biography—Juvenile literature. 3. Samurai—Japan—Biography—Juvenile literature. 4. Japan—History—Heian period, 794–1185—Juvenile literature. I. Hinds, Gareth, illustrator. II. Title.
DS856.72.M56T87 2015
952'.01092—dc23
[B]   2014049179

Printed in the United States of America
(hc)   10 9 8 7 6 5 4
(sc)   10 9 8 7 6 5 4 3

The art for this book was done in brush and ink with digital assist.
Display type set in Croteau and P22 Franklin Caslon
Text type set in Adobe Caslon Pro
Color separations by Colourscan Print Co Pte Ltd, Singapore
Printed by Berryville Graphics in Berryville, Virginia, USA
Production supervision by Brian G. Walker
Designed by Susan Mallory Sherman

CONTENTS

CHARACTERS AND PLACES

Please note that in Japanese the *r* sound is very soft; the pronunciation is actually somewhere between an *r* and an *l*. A vowel with a line over it indicates a drawn-out sound. For example, *ō* is pronounced like the long *o* sound in the English word *row*, but is held for a beat longer. In general, Japanese words do not have a stressed syllable.

THE MINAMOTO

Yoshitsune (yoh-shee-tsoo-nay): *our main character*

Yoritomo (yoh-ree-toh-moh): *Yoshitsune's elder half brother and leader of the Minamoto samurai*

Noriyori (noh-ree-yoh-ree): *another half brother of Yoshitsune*

Kiso Yoshinaka (kee-soh yoh-shee-nah-kah): *Yoshitsune's cousin*

Yukiie (yoo-kee-ee-ay): *Yoshitsune's uncle*

Tametomo (tah-may-toh-moh): *Yoshitsune's uncle; famous archer who commits first known seppuku (ritual suicide)*

Yoshiie (yoh-shee-ee-ay): *Yoshitsune's great-grandfather; a famous barbarian-fighter*

Yorimasa (yoh-ree-mah-sah): *distant relation of Yoshitsune; commits seppuku*

Tokiwa (toh-kee-wah): *Yoshitsune's mother*

Yoshitomo (yoh-shee-toh-moh): *Yoshitsune's father*

THE TAIRA

Kiyomori (kee-yoh-moh-ree): *leader of the Taira samurai*
Noritsune (noh-ree-tsoo-nay): *Kiyomori's nephew and a famous archer*
Munemori (moo-nay-moh-ree): *son of Kiyomori and leader of the Taira after his father's death*
Atsumori (ah-tsoo-moh-ree): *Kiyomori's nephew*

THE IMPERIAL FAMILY

Go-Shirakawa (goh shee-rah-kah-wah): *the Retired Emperor and head of the imperial family*
Antoku (ahn-toh-koo): *Go-Shirakawa's grandson; emperor of Japan*
Mochihito (moh-chee-hee-toh): *one of Go-Shirakawa's sons*

THE HIRAIZUMI FUJIWARA

Hidehira (hee-day-hee-rah): *lord of Hiraizumi*
Yasuhira (yah-soo-hee-rah): *Hidehira's heir*
Tadahira (tah-dah-hee-rah): *younger son of Hidehira*

YOSHITSUNE'S FRIENDS

Benkei (ben-kay): *a warrior-monk*
Ise Saburō (ee-say sah-boo-roh): *a reformed bandit*
Shizuka (shee-zoo-kah): *famous dancer and Yoshitsune's lover*
Tadanobu (tah-dah-noh-boo): *a samurai from Hiraizumi*
Tsuginobu (tsoo-gee-noh-boo): *a samurai from Hiraizumi; Tadanobu's brother*
Washinoo (wah-shee-no-oh): *a former mountain hunter*

OTHER CHARACTERS

Kagetoki (kah-gay-toh-kee): *Yoritomo's favorite retainer*
Shōshun (shoh-shoon): *Yoritomo's retainer*

PLACE NAMES

Biwa (bee-wah): *large lake near Kyoto*

Dan-no-Ura (dahn-noh-oo-rah): *naval battle site in the straits between the islands of Honshu and Kyushu*

Fuji (foo-jee) **River**: *battle site in central Japan*

Hiraizumi (hee-rye-zoo-mee): *elegant city in northern Japan*

Hiyodorigoe (hee-yoh-doh-ree-goh-ay) **Cliffs**: *steep slope behind the Taira fortress at Ichi-no-Tani*

Honshu (hohn-shoo): *main Japanese island*

Ichi-no-Tani (ee-chee-noh-tah-nee): *Taira fortification on the Settsu coast, near modern-day Kobe*

Ikuta-no-Mori (ee-koo-tah-noh-moh-ree): *Taira fortification on the Settsu coast, near modern-day Kobe*

Kamakura (kah-mah-koo-rah): *Yoritomo's headquarters in eastern Japan*

Koshigoe (koh-shee-goh-ay): *small town near Kamakura*

Kurama (koo-rah-mah): *temple north of Kyoto*

Kyoto (kyoh-toh): *capital of Japan*

Kyushu (kyoo-shoo): *large Japanese island off the western coast of Honshu*

Seta (say-tah): *small town east of Kyoto, site of a major bridge*

Settsu (set-tsoo) **Coast**: *coastline southwest of Kyoto, near modern-day Kobe and Osaka*

Shikoku (shee-koh-koo): *large Japanese island off the southwest coast of Honshu*

Uji (oo-jee) **River**: *major river flowing out of Lake Biwa*

Yashima (yah-shee-mah): *island off the coast of Shikoku*

Yoshino (yoh-shee-noh) **Mountains**: *rugged area south of Kyoto*

MAP OF JAPAN

SEA OF JAPAN (East Sea)

**SEA OF JAPAN
(EAST SEA)**

LAKE
BIWA

Ichi-no-Tani

KYOTO

2

1

Uji Riv

4
Dan-no-Ura

SEA

3 *Yashima*

YOSHINO MOU

INLAND

Shikoku

Kyushu

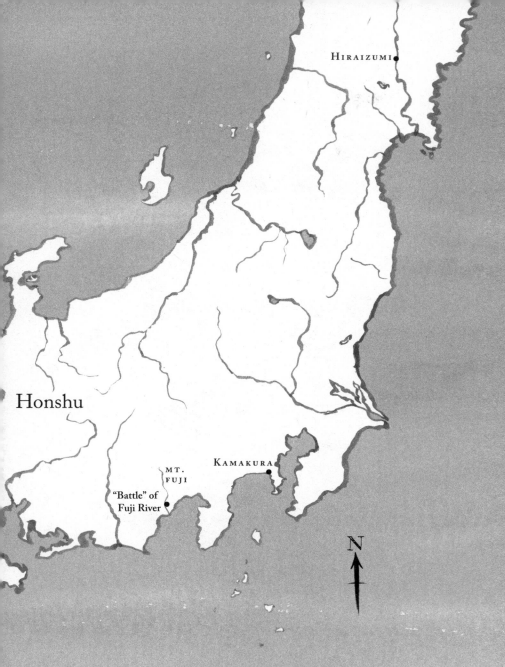

HIRAIZUMI •

Honshu

MT.
FUJI

KAMAKURA •

"Battle" of
Fuji River •

N

PACIFIC OCEAN

Detail Maps

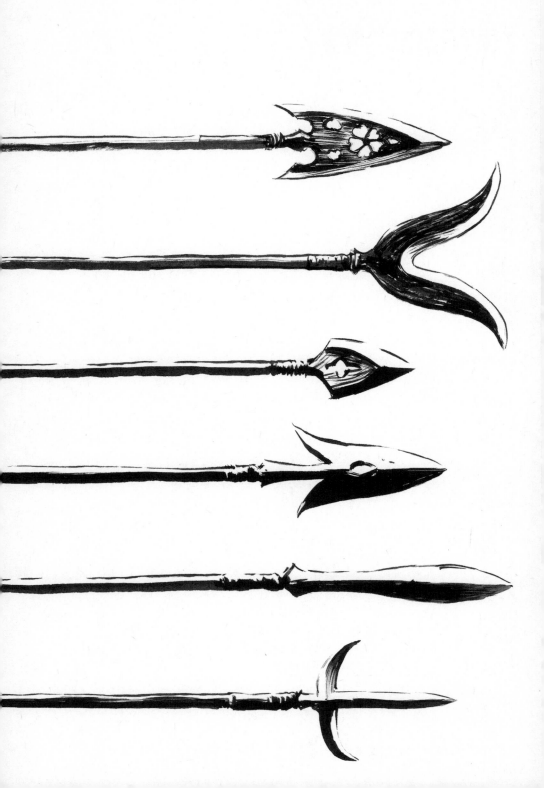

INTRODUCTION

*Few warriors are as famous as the Japanese samurai. We
remember those beautiful swords and those fearsome helmets.
We recall, with both horror and fascination, how some chose to
end their own lives. But no one can understand the samurai
without knowing Minamoto Yoshitsune.*

*Yoshitsune's story unfolds in the late twelfth century,
during the adolescence of the samurai. Yes, cultures have their
youth, maturity, and old age, just as people do. During Yoshitsune's lifetime the samurai awakened. Their culture was bold,
rebellious, and eager to flex its muscle. The samurai would
ultimately destroy Japan's old way of life and forge a new one
using fire and steel and pain.*

*Yoshitsune was at the very heart of this samurai rising.
Exile, runaway, fugitive, rebel, and hero, he became the most
famous warrior in Japanese history. The reason is simple:
Yoshitsune was the kind of man other samurai longed to be.*

DISASTER IN KYOTO

Kyoto, 1160

Minamoto Yoshitsune's inheritance arrived early. The boy could not yet walk when his father left him a lost war, a shattered family, and a bitter enemy.

Yoshitsune's father prepared for battle in the cold darkness of a winter night. Warrior pride demanded elegance, so servants led out two warhorses—one black and one white—for him to choose between. He ordered pine torches held aloft. The bronze and silver fittings on the horses' saddles flashed and sparkled in the light.

"When one goes into battle, nothing is so important as one's horse," Yoshitsune's father declared.

Yoshitsune's father was the leader of the Minamoto samurai. Five hundred warriors followed him as he rode, astride his black warhorse, through the shadowy streets of Kyoto. Surely the commoners who lived along the way— fishmongers and silk weavers, carpenters and midwives, beggars and papermakers—were awakened by the clattering of two thousand hooves. Just as surely they clutched their children close and remained silent, knowing that nothing good ever comes of heavily armed men moving in the dead of night.

Two hours after midnight, Yoshitsune's father and his men reached their target: the palace of the Retired Emperor. The Minamoto forces barged through the palace gates, dragged the startled Retired Emperor from his slumber, and shoved him into an oxcart. The cart rolled away with Yoshitsune's father riding guard alongside.

Never before had a samurai dared to lay hands on a former emperor. As head of the imperial family, the Retired Emperor wielded enormous power. The reigning emperor—the Retired Emperor's teenage son—served as a figurehead. The Retired Emperor was the true ruler: he wrote the laws, controlled the government, and awarded titles and land to the Japanese elite.

In addition to his power, the Retired Emperor enjoyed enormous prestige. Japanese emperors were considered semidivine descendants of the sun goddess. Most people would think twice about kidnapping a demigod, but Yoshitsune's father was not a think-twice sort of person. Plus he was in a nasty snit. A few years earlier, he had taken the Retired Emperor's side in a political dispute. When the Retired Emperor won the dispute, Yoshitsune's father had expected a lofty title and the wealth that went with it. Instead, he was named Minister of the Stables of the Left. A rival samurai leader named Taira Kiyomori, who had also backed the Retired Emperor, received a much grander reward.

To get back at those who had slighted him, Yoshitsune's

father was willing to risk his own life, the lives of his men, and the lives of his children. He hoped that by kidnapping the Retired Emperor, he could seize control of Japan. He planned to force the Retired Emperor to heap titles on him while stripping them away from Taira Kiyomori. But first Yoshitsune's father wanted the Retired Emperor to know just how angry he was about that "Minister of the Stables of the Left" business. He ordered his men to burn the Retired Emperor's palace.

The Minamoto samurai set the wooden buildings ablaze. They lined the avenues outside the palace gates and drew their bows. Everyone who tried to escape was shot down, whether nobleman, lady-in-waiting, or servant boy.

A war chronicle says: "If they sought to avoid the arrows, they were consumed by fire. Those who quailed before the arrows and were terrified by the fire jumped into a well. But those on the bottom drowned in the water, and those on top were buried by ash and embers from the multitude of buildings burning in the violent wind, and not a single one of them was saved."

As smoke and screams filled the air around the flaming palace, news of the attack spread. Yoshitsune's father had waited for his nemesis Taira Kiyomori to leave town before kidnapping the Retired Emperor. But as soon as messengers reached Kiyomori, the Taira lord readied to ride to the Retired Emperor's defense.

Kiyomori dressed in black-laced armor and black bearskin boots and carried a black-lacquer scabbard and black-lacquered arrows. From his helmet rose a brilliant silver ornament shaped like monstrous beetle horns. Mounted on a thickly muscled black horse, the dark knight of Kyoto galloped home.

Other Taira samurai rushed to their leader's side. By the time Kiyomori reached the capital, he had gathered three hundred warriors. Yoshitsune's father and his five hundred followers had taken over another imperial palace in Kyoto. Taira Kiyomori led the counterattack. Despite a fierce fight, the outnumbered Taira were unable to dislodge the Minamoto.

Kiyomori and his men began to withdraw. Yoshitsune's father assumed that the Taira were retreating toward Kiyomori's mansion east of the city, and he couldn't resist the temptation to crush his archrival. He ordered his warriors into pursuit.

As soon as the Minamoto left the safety of the palace walls, squads of Taira attacked from all sides. The "retreat" had been a ruse; the Taira had simply circled around the block. Arrows sliced in from every direction. Unable to retreat, the Minamoto samurai were stamped out like the embers of a dying fire.

Meanwhile, the Retired Emperor was being held prisoner at an imperial library elsewhere in Kyoto. He disguised himself as a common gentleman, walked past his Minamoto guards, and fled into the snow-frosted hills. The entire war was now entirely pointless.

Yoshitsune's father had ridden to war with his two eldest sons, a nineteen-year-old and a sixteen-year-old. During the battle outside the palace, the older boy fought bravely but was captured by Kiyomori's men. The younger boy suffered a deep arrow wound in his knee. Yoshitsune's father and his wounded son, protected by a small band of loyal warriors, managed to break through the Taira lines. They rode east toward the Minamoto homeland.

Yoshitsune's father planned to gather reinforcements

and return to battle. But as they rode, his wounded son's condition grew steadily worse. At last, unable to go on, the boy begged to be killed.

His father obliged.

At last Yoshitsune's father and his remaining men stopped to rest at the home of a retainer (a lower-ranking samurai who had pledged his service and loyalty). But pledging is one thing; true loyalty is another. This retainer didn't want to be allied with a loser. He offered Yoshitsune's father a bath, which was gratefully accepted. The retainer's men then burst into the bathroom and murdered Yoshitsune's father. Only his head returned to Kyoto.

The bloody trophy was tied to a sandalwood tree beside the Kyoto prison gate. There it rotted, a sharp reminder that when you go into battle, the most important thing isn't selecting your horse. The most important thing is *winning*.

But Taira Kiyomori wasn't satisfied with his enemy's death. He also wanted his enemy's sons. Kiyomori now held both the nineteen-year-old who had fought in the battle and a fourteen-year-old who hadn't ridden to war. Kiyomori had the older boy beheaded but hadn't yet decided what to do with the younger boy.

The Taira lord knew that Yoshitsune's father (who, like other well-born Japanese men, had multiple wives) also had three young sons by a wife named Tokiwa. Tokiwa had a seven-year-old boy, a five-year-old boy, and a baby named Yoshitsune. Despite their youth and innocence, Taira Kiyomori wanted those sons as well. After all, samurai boys would grow up to bear swords—and grudges.

Tokiwa knew this, too. As soon as she learned of her

husband's death, she fled Kyoto with Yoshitsune bundled against her chest and his older brothers clutching her robes. Frost paralyzed the trees and ice stilled the rivers as they stumbled, half-blind, through clouding snow.

When they reached Tokiwa's relatives in a nearby town, terrible news awaited: Kiyomori had arrested Tokiwa's mother and was torturing her to find out where Tokiwa and her sons were hiding. In hopes of saving her mother but terrified for her sons, Tokiwa led her children back to Kyoto. The forlorn family surrendered at the gates of Kiyomori's mansion.

Triumphant Kiyomori could not resist a peek at his dead rival's wife. After all, Tokiwa's looks were legendary. It was said she had arrived in Kyoto as a teenager to compete for the position of imperial lady-in-waiting. Out of a thousand pretty girls, the hundred most lovely were chosen, and then the ten most radiant, and finally the most beautiful of all: Tokiwa.

And so Yoshitsune's mother, the twelfth-century beauty queen, was brought before Kiyomori, victorious samurai lord. Tokiwa clutched little Yoshitsune to her chest and begged Kiyomori to kill her first.

"Every mother, high or low, wanders in darkness for love of her children," Tokiwa said, tears raining down her face. "I know that I could not live a moment longer without them."

Maybe Kiyomori felt a stirring of Buddhist compassion. Maybe something else moved the samurai as he gazed upon Tokiwa, so dazzling, so desperate. What harm, Kiyomori must have reasoned, could come of mercy? Tokiwa's fatherless children needn't become warriors. The older ones could be sent to Buddhist temples and trained as monks. In a few years baby Yoshitsune could follow the same quiet path. Why not? After all, the Taira had won the war. Surely the scattered sons of the Minamoto—and little Yoshitsune in particular—could pose no possible threat.

Kiyomori was wrong. Utterly, fatally wrong.

2

HEADLESS GHOSTS

KURAMA, 1160–1174

We know very little about Yoshitsune's early life. According to some accounts, Tokiwa became Kiyomori's mistress. As a small child Yoshitsune may have spent his first years in Kiyomori's household on the outskirts of Kyoto.

In those days Kyoto was the center of the Japanese universe. The emperor lived there, hidden like a nesting doll inside his palace, which was surrounded by a compound, which was surrounded by a city laid out as tidily as a checkerboard. Such a special place required spiritual protection. As everyone knew, bad luck and ill spirits often arrived from a northerly direction, so Kyoto had been built on a plain sheltered on the north, east, and west by mountains. Tile-roofed temples sprouted like mushroom caps from the forested slopes, providing an extra line of defense against evil demons, malicious sprites, and vengeful spirits. And a good thing, too. The recent Minamoto-Taira conflict had sharply increased the number of bad-tempered ghosts wafting around.

At about age seven Yoshitsune was taken away from Tokiwa and delivered to one of the holy places north of Kyoto. Did no one notice that Kurama Temple was dedicated to Bishamon-ten, the Buddhist patron god of warriors?

At Kurama there were no soft laps and mother's kisses. Yoshitsune entered a world of hard floorboards and silent statues. The temple offered no chairs, no beds, and no bedding. Monks and monks-in-training slept on thin straw mats and instead of blankets covered themselves with extra clothing made of rough hemp. No roaring fireplaces warmed the wooden buildings, not even in the frozen core of winter.

The monks of Kurama expected young apprentices to memorize the names and proper worship of Japan's divine beings. This wasn't easy. Buddhism had moved into Japan six centuries earlier but never evicted the gods of the native Shinto religion, so the invisible realm was rather crowded. There were cosmic Buddhas and Buddhist gods of salvation. Every major family had its own patron god, every hamlet had its local Buddha, and countless Shinto nature spirits inhabited oddly shaped rocks and stately trees.

Monks kept these divine beings happy by reciting and copying sacred Buddhist scriptures. As part of their religious training, boys like Yoshitsune spent countless leg-numbing hours kneeling over sheets and scrolls of rice paper, learning to read and write scriptures in both

Japanese (the everyday language) and Chinese (the language of scholars and administrators).

Besides pleasing the gods, Buddha's sacred words also worked magic on the souls of the dead. Buddhists believed that a person's soul would be reborn into a new body and that the balance of good deeds and bad deeds in one's prior life determined one's fate in this one. However, while awaiting its next reincarnation, a soul sometimes lingered in the world as a ghost. Unhappy ghosts caused illness and accidents, so it was very important to keep departed souls placid until their next rebirth. As a monk, Yoshitsune would be expected to copy and recite scriptures to soothe the restless spirits of his dead relatives. The restlessness of the boy's own spirit was apparently overlooked.

No boy with Yoshitsune's energy could be contained within incense-scented walls. Kurama's doors opened to a wilderness of tumbling waterfalls and lofty cedars, pink-faced monkeys and flying squirrels. Short-winged hawks chased smaller birds through the forest, crashing recklessly through bushes in fierce pursuit, like samurai on the wing.

People later told stories about Yoshitsune's boyhood and how he sought out the secrecy of the forest. They said he pretended that bushes were Taira and slashed the enemy shrubbery with switches and sticks, saving his most ferocious attacks for a tree he named Kiyomori.

Of course, Yoshitsune couldn't possibly remember what had happened in Kyoto. He was just a baby during that terrible time. Yet even hidden away at Kurama, he learned something of his family history. Stories travel. Even holy men gossip.

In Yoshitsune's time the names Minamoto and Taira were famous throughout Japan. Yoshitsune was probably proud to discover that he was the tenth-generation descendant of an emperor. His enemy Taira Kiyomori also boasted an imperial bloodline. The ancestors of both Yoshitsune and Kiyomori had become samurai because of the problem of excess princes.

Japanese emperors often married several wives and produced more sons than necessary to carry on the imperial line. Unfortunately, within the strict ranking system of the imperial court, only a limited number of high-ranking titles (which came with vast estates and equally vast riches) were available to these princes. Sons born to the emperor's lower-ranking wives had little chance of advancement, so they sometimes went looking for opportunities outside Kyoto. The founders of the Taira and Minamoto families were spare heirs who moved to the provinces to seek their fortunes. The Minamoto family became a power in the east; the Taira dominated the west.

As provincial lords, these princes (and their descendants) took care of the messy parts of governing. They caught criminals, killed barbarians, and forced peasants to pay taxes. Sometimes they owned their own land, but mostly they acted as estate managers for higher-ranking aristocrats living in Kyoto. The aristocrats in the capital didn't want to get their robes muddy. They preferred to concentrate on poetry, fashion, and illicit love affairs with one another's wives and daughters.

In the provinces, the Minamoto and Taira lords commanded great respect because of their imperial blood. Well-off local men became their retainers. The Minamoto and Taira also kept in close contact with the capital. However, the snobbish aristocrats of Kyoto never let the samurai forget who was who in the social scheme. If transported into a modern high school, the Kyoto nobility would consider themselves the cool kids. They thought of the samurai as dumb jocks.

As the years passed, the Minamoto and Taira grew in wealth and military muscle. The two great samurai families served the imperial family, it is said, "like the two wings of a bird." They put down rebellions, kept the roads and sea routes safe from bandits and pirates, and made sure that taxes flowed into Kyoto. Yet as the power of the samurai lords increased, so did their inferiority complex. And there is nothing in the world as dangerous as a man bristling with weapons and insecurities.

When Yoshitsune's father kidnapped the Retired Emperor and burned his palace, he thought his actions would make the Minamoto stronger and more secure. His bungling produced the opposite result. Before the failed rebellion, the Retired Emperor had kept the growing influence of the samurai in check by playing one samurai family off against the other, Minamoto versus Taira. But now the Minamoto were weak and leaderless, unable to serve as a counterweight to the power of the Taira family. Taira Kiyomori had the upper hand. He forced the Retired Emperor to appoint him chancellor—the highest rank ever awarded to a samurai. Titles, land, and wealth flowed to Kiyomori, his family, and his friends. Team Taira was on top.

This bitter news surely reached Kurama Temple. It's easy to imagine young Yoshitsune, angry and frustrated, slashing his way through forests of phantom Taira. But how could a temple boy redeem the Minamoto family's honor?

Yoshitsune didn't have money. Or allies. Or anyone

who could teach him essential samurai skills: archery, horsemanship, and swordsmanship. He wasn't big or strong or good-looking. The only description we have of him is "a small, pale youth with crooked teeth and bulging eyes." Maybe it's a blessing that the mirrors of the time were made of polished metal and not very reflective.

Yoshitsune couldn't hope for rescue. Most of his surviving uncles and cousins lived far to the east under the beady gaze of Taira overlords. He did have at least one surviving half brother—the boy who had been fourteen at the time of the disaster in Kyoto. But his half brother, now a grown man, was held captive by one of Kiyomori's retainers. Yoshitsune's two full brothers—the other sons of Tokiwa—had already become monks. It was the path Kiyomori had chosen for Yoshitsune as well.

Yoshitsune's only assets were brains, ambition, and a dream. But childhood dreams can change history.

His fifteenth birthday loomed. At this age Japanese boys were considered men. Soon Yoshitsune would be expected to shave his head and take his final religious vows. A safe life of scripture reading and ghost soothing unscrolled before him.

That spring a wealthy gold merchant stopped at Kurama on his way north. The gold merchant turned out to be a friend of the Minamoto and was willing to help. Yoshitsune seized his chance to change his fate. Disguised as the merchant's servant, he slipped away.

Surely Yoshitsune understood the risk. His escape was no boyish game; it was a rebellion against Taira Kiyomori, the most powerful samurai in Japan. If Yoshitsune were captured, his severed head would probably dangle from the sandalwood tree beside the Kyoto prison gate. Just like his father's.

Eight centuries separate us from Yoshitsune. Yet it is easy to imagine the hope and fear in his heart as he launched himself into a dangerous world.

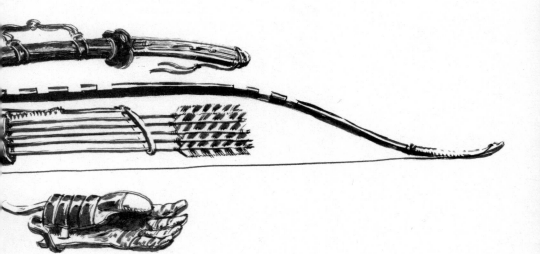

3

SAMURAI BOOT CAMP

Hᴵʀᴀɪᴢᴜᴍɪ, 1174–1180

Where could Yoshitsune go? He couldn't escape to western Japan—that was Taira country. He couldn't remain near Kyoto, because Taira Kiyomori controlled the capital. And Kiyomori's allies now ruled the Minamoto homeland to the east.

His only shred of hope lay north. Six hundred miles away, on the edge of civilization, a semi-independent samurai lord lived in a beautiful city made wealthy by gold mined from the surrounding mountains. Fabled Hiraizumi was half Shangri-la, half El Dorado.

Hiraizumi had been built by a branch of the influential Fujiwara family. Like the founders of the Minamoto and Taira, the founder of the Hiraizumi Fujiwara had left Kyoto to seek his fortune. In the north he struck gold—literally.

Unfortunately for Yoshitsune, previous generations of the Minamoto and Hiraizumi Fujiwara families had clashed. The lords of Hiraizumi knew that the Minamoto had always looked to the north with a greedy glint in their eyes. Would the lord of Hiraizumi welcome Yoshitsune, a Minamoto fugitive? Or would he instead choose to curry favor with powerful Kiyomori? Maybe he would send Yoshitsune back to Kyoto bound and gagged. Or maybe he would save on transport costs and just send Yoshitsune's head.

However the lord of Hiraizumi might react, Yoshitsune had no better option. So the gold merchant and his "servant" followed the network of roads (often no more than muddy tracks) that linked Japan's provinces. Their path took them over mountain passes and through valleys quilted by rice paddies. In those days of late spring and summer, the fields were so brilliantly green it almost hurt the eyes.

They passed villages and, occasionally, the homes of rural samurai. The peasants, whose endless labor supported the lifestyles of the rich and well armed, lived in dirt-floored huts set on drier ground above their fields. Their samurai overlords lived in complexes of wooden buildings protected by moats and mud-and-timber walls. Defensive fortifications were a necessity. Private wars sometimes broke out between neighboring samurai, and family feuds could turn violent. Inheritance disputes between half brothers were sometimes resolved through murder.

Yoshitsune and the gold merchant probably avoided samurai whenever they could. After all, Kiyomori had eyes and ears everywhere. Unfortunately they couldn't avoid barrier stations. At these government checkpoints, guards inspected travelers and goods moving along the roads. Yoshitsune had to rely on his servant disguise to avoid attracting attention. Luckily for Yoshitsune, twelfth-century Japan lacked photographs, newspapers, and WANTED: DEAD OR ALIVE posters.

After a long day of travel—and the stress of deceiving checkpoint guards—the homey smell of wood smoke probably drew the weary travelers to wayside inns. The appeal wasn't just a dry mat to sleep on or a pot of hot rice gruel. Inns attracted a wandering underclass of puppeteers, storytellers, jugglers, dancers, singers, and women with bad reputations—*exactly* the sort of riffraff parents warn their children to stay away from.

Imagine Yoshitsune's delight.

The teenage runaway probably watched, mouth agape, as entertainers performed the popular tales of his time. In these stories wrestlers battle snakes and sharks; a young warrior discovers that a pretty girl is really a shape-shifting fox; a mother becomes a demon and tries to eat her children. In one tale a boy avenges his father's death by stealing a sword and killing his father's murderer as he sleeps. This was an act, the storytellers assured listeners, approved by heaven.

Along the way Yoshitsune probably heard a few stories about his own famous family. His great-grandfather Minamoto Yoshiie was only eighteen when he began his career as a barbarian killer. "None of his arrows left his bow in vain, and every target hit toppled over dead," the storytellers claimed. "He dashed about like lightning and flew like wind, his divine military prowess known to all."

No pressure, Yoshitsune.

In addition to a superhuman great-grandfather, Yoshitsune had an action-hero uncle. It is said that Minamoto Tametomo was such a strong archer that he could kill two men with a single shot. During one battle Tametomo's arrow went straight through his enemy's armored body and sunk deep into the man's saddle, pinning the dying man to his horse. Once, while successfully defending a gate (alone, of course) against 150 attackers, Uncle Tametomo boasted, "Let there be a thousand men or ten thousand against me, I'll shoot them all down."

Tametomo's death was just as supersized as his life. Several years before Yoshitsune's birth, the great warrior ran afoul of those in power and was banished from Kyoto. As a parting blow Uncle Tametomo's shoulders were dislocated—a particularly horrible punishment for a great archer. He couldn't even hold a fan, much less the reins of a horse.

His captors built a cage to carry Tametomo to his place of exile. "You men probably think I am finished," Tametomo said. "Well, just watch!" He rocked his body so furiously that he smashed through the cage.

Recaptured, Tametomo finally arrived at his place of banishment—a distant island. Eventually he recovered the use of his arms. He claimed that the maiming had lengthened his bow arm and given him a better draw.

In exile Uncle Tametomo turned enthusiastically to piracy. Four years before Yoshitsune escaped Kurama, the Retired Emperor (the same one kidnapped by Yoshitsune's father) ordered a large posse of samurai to invade the island and execute Tametomo.

Despite the odds against him, Tametomo fought furiously. Finally, surrounded by attackers and facing certain defeat, he loosed his last arrow. Then he walked back into his house, set his back against a pillar, and cut his belly open with the point of his sword. Tametomo's extraordinary life ended at age thirty-one.

Why had Tametomo cut his own stomach? Warriors dreaded a gaping abdominal wound more than any other injury. Death was certain—but it took an agonizingly long time to arrive. Samurai sometimes took their own lives, but none had ever killed himself in such a spectacularly horrible fashion. Had Tametomo lost his sanity? Or was he making one last over-the-top statement about his manliness, his determination, his unconquerable spirit?

No one knew for sure. But whatever his state of mind, Tametomo's manner of death made a deep and lasting impression.

After several months on the road, Yoshitsune and the gold merchant reached Hiraizumi. The exquisite city stretched across a well-watered plain between two rivers. Shops, storehouses, and residences crowded the prosperous commercial center; finely crafted pagodas and temples decorated the surrounding hills. The jewel in Hiraizumi's crown was the Hall of Gold—a shimmering shrine completely covered, inside and out, with gold leaf and mother-of-pearl.

Yoshitsune, his heart no doubt thudding in his chest, presented himself to the lord of Hiraizumi. Fujiwara Hidehira didn't kill Yoshitsune or send him away. Was it pity or admiration? The scrawny boy certainly had courage. Whatever his reason, Hidehira welcomed the Minamoto runaway into his own household. By all accounts he treated Yoshitsune like one of his own six sons.

Once more Yoshitsune's life changed abruptly. He probably lived in Hidehira's mansion, an airy complex of residences linked by roofed walkways and artfully arranged around gardens and artificial lakes. Yoshitsune traded his servant clothes of humble hemp for robes and wide-legged trousers of sumptuous silk. No longer would he be expected to spend his days seeking divine favor and soothing ghosts. Hidehira, like other wealthy Japanese, paid the monks of the city's temples to handle his family's spiritual protection. This being snazzy Hiraizumi, the monks pleased the gods, ghosts, and spirits with sacred words inked in gold and silver on paper dyed midnight blue.

Yet Yoshitsune hadn't come to Hiraizumi for its elegance. He had come to learn the way of the samurai. No amount of glitz and gold could make that an easy task.

In Yoshitsune's day samurai were primarily mounted archers. Because archery was a complex skill requiring years of intense practice, samurai boys began training at age six or seven. All the men and boys in a samurai household drilled, over and over, until drawing an arrow and shooting from the back of a galloping horse became as natural and unthinking as breathing. These close-knit squads of samurai practiced until they could coordinate their attacks (and defend one another's backs) with uncanny precision. After nine or ten years of training, a fifteen- or sixteen-year-old samurai was considered ready for war.

And now Yoshitsune, an unskilled teenager, had arrived in Hiraizumi wanting to be a warrior! It was like a boy who had never played Little League showing up for spring training with the Yankees.

First Yoshitsune had to learn how to shoot. Japanese bows were seven to nine feet long and made of bamboo, mulberry wood, and lacquer. The bow's handgrip was not in the middle (as in Western archery) but placed one-third of the way up. This made it easier to swing the bow over the horse's neck. A samurai reached behind his back to pull an arrow from his quiver, nocked his arrow, then raised his bow over his head; he drew his bow while lowering his arrow to eye level. Japanese archery was difficult enough to master when standing still. Careening along on a galloping horse made it even harder.

Yoshitsune probably didn't have much experience with warhorses before he arrived at Hiraizumi. Only a superb rider could guide a galloping stallion with his legs or voice while simultaneously shooting arrows. It didn't help that the small, shaggy beasts preferred by Japanese samurai were notorious for their bad attitudes. The most famous warhorse of Yoshitsune's time was named Ikezuki ("Bad-Tempered Biter").

If firing arrows while trying to control a cranky stallion wasn't difficult enough, Yoshitsune had to do it while wearing a helmet and armor. Samurai armor was made of plates of lacquer-covered leather and metal that overlapped like roof tiles to protect against hailstorms of enemy arrows. The plates were laced together by leather thongs and—for wealthy samurai—colorful silk cords. Samurai didn't carry a shield while on horseback, since they needed both hands to draw their bow. Instead, they relied on giant shoulder flaps. The flaps could be pulled forward when riding into an onslaught of arrows but were rigged to fall back when the samurai lifted his arms to shoot.

Samurai chest armor had two pieces: a single panel tied to the warrior's right side and a three-sided wraparound panel that covered the rest of his torso. However, the bulky chest armor didn't fit close to the body and the weight of the pieces wasn't perfectly balanced. The armor tended to shift suddenly from side to side, especially on a fast-moving horse. Yoshitsune, a slightly built young man wrestling with forty to sixty pounds of armor, probably hit the dirt more than once.

Of course, a samurai also carried a sword.

A twelfth-century samurai's main weapon was his bow, but his sword offered a last line of defense if he ran out of arrows or was knocked off his horse. Yet even as a backup weapon the sword carried a symbolic weight that the bow did not. Weapons like bows and spears were also used for hunting. The sword had a singular purpose: to end human life.

At first Yoshitsune probably practiced with a wooden sword. Though it lacked a cutting edge, a wooden weapon could still break bones and wound flesh. Yoshitsune no doubt spent a great deal of time feeling like one aching bruise. But as his skills sharpened, he probably began practicing with a real blade.

In Yoshitsune's time the traditional samurai sword was the *tachi*: a long, curved blade sheathed edge-down and hung from the left hip. The tachi would eventually develop into the *katana*, the classic samurai sword. Lighter and shorter than the tachi, the katana could be wielded in one hand or two. And because it was worn at the waist and sheathed edge-up (rather than edge-down), the drawing of the katana could be turned into a powerful overhand strike. This was crucial. Sneak attacks were standard operating procedure for samurai, and a swiftly drawn sword could save a warrior's life.

Once a tachi or katana was drawn, its sharp tip could be used for stabbing. However, a Japanese sword was primarily designed to slash. The blade's graceful curve wasn't an artistic statement—it was a deadly feat of engineering. The curve distributed the force of the samurai's strike along the entire arc of the razored edge. A strong blow severed bone and opened gaping wounds that were often fatal.

Modern experts consider Japanese swords the finest

bladed weapons ever created. For a twelfth-century samurai like Yoshitsune, his sword was the very latest in dismemberment technology.

Yoshitsune's skills gradually improved. The lush meadows and woodlands around Hiraizumi offered abundant hunting, and during the fall and winter he and his friends probably rode out to shoot birds—fast-moving targets to challenge the skills of the finest archers. "Shining for deer" offered another way of practicing the arts of war. Shining involved hunting at night with torches and shooting arrows at the eerie reflection of the deer's eyes. Samurai like Yoshitsune sometimes needed to kill in the dark.

News occasionally arrived from the capital, where the rise of the Taira seemed unstoppable. Taira Kiyomori had recruited three hundred youths as his spies and sent them out to terrorize Kyoto. If anyone was overhead speaking ill of Kiyomori, the young brutes broke into his home, seized his belongings, and dragged him off to jail.

Kiyomori even had power over Retired Emperor Go-Shirakawa (the man who had been kidnapped by Yoshitsune's father). Kiyomori forced Go-Shirakawa to agree to a marriage between Kiyomori's seventeen-year-old daughter and Go-Shirakawa's eleven-year-old son, the new reigning emperor. Some years later Kiyomori's daughter gave birth to a boy. Little Antoku was named crown prince.

The Kyoto aristocrats found this situation repellent. It wasn't the age difference between bride and groom that made them shudder—it was the thoroughly nauseating notion of a crown prince with samurai blood. In the Japanese imperial tradition, the title of crown prince didn't automatically go to the eldest son of the current emperor; the crown prince was chosen from among all the living sons of reigning and retired emperors. Everyone knew that Retired Emperor Go-Shirakawa had plenty of other sons and grandsons with "purer" pedigrees than Crown Prince Antoku.

In the spring of 1180, Kiyomori's spies told him that the Retired Emperor was plotting against him. Go-Shirakawa was placed under arrest. Kiyomori forced the reigning emperor (now a teenager) to give up his throne and had Crown Prince Antoku named emperor of Japan. This power grab was too much for one of Go-Shirakawa's adult sons, Prince Mochihito. The prince issued an edict calling on other samurai to rise against the Taira:

> *In recent years the Taira have displayed contempt for imperial rule and utter lack of respect for the way of good government. . . . For this reason go forth now and, with the gods' help and in conformity with this decree, chastise the [Taira] and disperse the enemies of the imperial line. The time has come: Exercise now the martial prowess to which you are heir, . . . distinguish yourself, and exalt the honor of your house.*

Prince Mochihito knew that Kiyomori would probably react violently to being named an enemy of the state. The rebel prince sought protection from the only prominent Minamoto who remained in Kyoto: seventy-four-year-old Minamoto Yorimasa, a courtier who was a distant relative of Yoshitsune's.

Twenty years earlier, when Yoshitsune was a baby, Yorimasa had wisely refused to join Yoshitsune's father in his rebellion. As a result he hadn't been punished and had remained in Kyoto. Due to the quality of his poetry (the skill that really mattered at court), he was awarded a high-ranking title. Yorimasa had been on good terms with Kiyomori for many years, but now he felt that the Taira leader had gone too far. Yorimasa agreed to support Prince Mochihito's rebellion.

Yorimasa, the elderly warrior-poet, and Mochihito, the imperial prince, had gathered only a small force when Kiyomori's samurai caught them on the banks of the Uji River south of Kyoto. During the battle that followed, Prince Mochihito was killed. Yorimasa's three sons also died. Of the rebels it is said "their corpses bleached on the mosses of the ancient bank; their lives flowed away on the waves of the great stream."

Wounded by an arrow in the leg, all hope lost, old Yorimasa limped to the Phoenix Hall, a graceful Chinese-style temple on the riverbank. Beneath the winged edges of its roof, he wrote his last poem:

> *This forgotten tree*
> *never through the fleeting years*
> *burst into flower,*
> *and now that the end has come,*
> *no thought but turns to sorrow.*

Minamoto Yorimasa set down his brush. Then he picked up his sword and plunged it into his belly, just as Tametomo had done. It was the second influential *seppuku*, or ritual suicide, in Japanese history.

The rebellion of Prince Mochihito and Yorimasa failed. Yet it ignited a second rebellion that would change Yoshitsune's life.

Nineteen years earlier, in the aftermath of the first Minamoto-Taira conflict, Kiyomori had spared one of Yoshitsune's half brothers. His name was Minamoto Yoritomo.

Yoritomo was only fourteen years old when his father had been killed and the Minamoto samurai defeated. Kiyomori ordered one of his retainers to keep the boy prisoner, and so Yoritomo was sent to the retainer's home in a province not far from the Minamoto homeland. As the hereditary leader of all Minamoto, Yoritomo lived on a sword's edge every day of his life. He knew that if Kiyomori ever felt threatened by a member of the Minamoto family, he would be the first to be executed.

Living in close quarters with one's jailer and his family does, however, offer special opportunities for advancement. Yoritomo eloped with the daughter of the man who was supposed to be guarding him. He was thirty-four years old and living quietly with his wife and in-laws when news arrived of the failed rebellion by Prince Mochihito and Minamoto Yorimasa. Yoritomo immediately realized the danger: he must fight or die.

Yoritomo convinced his father-in-law to switch sides. Using dead Prince Mochihito's edict as his justification, Yoritomo would proclaim himself the defender of the imperial family. Kiyomori would be painted as the evil usurper. Of course, Yoritomo's rebellion wouldn't survive any longer than Prince Mochihito's unless Yoritomo and his father-in-law could gather allies. Well-armed, welltrained allies.

A guppy in a shark tank would have better odds of

survival. But Yoritomo lacked options. The leader of the Minamoto sent out a call to all loyal samurai: join me in overthrowing the Taira!

When this stunning news reached Hiraizumi, Yoshitsune asked his foster father, Fujiwara Hidehira, for permission to ride south. Clearly Yoritomo needed warriors, and Yoshitsune had spent the last six years training for war. Fighting the Taira wasn't simply Yoshitsune's personal ambition. It was his duty as a Minamoto. He *had* to go—

Hidehira said no.

Yoshitsune now faced a wrenching choice. He owed everything to Hidehira. Instead of turning him over to Kiyomori, Hidehira had given Yoshitsune sanctuary and treated him like a member of the family. Hidehira had fed him, clothed him, armed him, and trained him. According to Japanese custom, a son should obey his father.

Yet Yoshitsune had another family. Although he couldn't remember much (if anything) about them, he was still a Minamoto.

Sometime in the fall of 1180, twenty-one-year-old Yoshitsune gathered his armor and weapons and slipped quietly out of Hiraizumi. However scrawny he might have been, however shaky his samurai skills, Yoshitsune knew that he carried the blood of great fighters like Great-Grandfather Yoshiie and Uncle Tametomo in his veins.

He rode south, alone, toward a land crumbling into civil war.

4

BROTHERS-IN-ARMS

KAMAKURA, 1180–1184

As Yoshitsune traveled south toward Yoritomo, Yoritomo
was simply trying to stay alive.

The Minamoto and their traditional allies were slow
to respond to Yoritomo's call to arms. And no wonder.
Over the past twenty years, many had developed friendly
relations with their Taira overlords. What did Yoritomo
have to offer? Yes, he was the hereditary leader of the
Minamoto. But he didn't hold a court title, own any land,
or control any wealth. Despite these considerable disad-
vantages, Yoritomo did possess two gifts. The first was in-
telligence. The second was the ability to say the most
outrageous things with a straight face.

Yoritomo sent out messages to the samurai of the
east, Minamoto and Taira alike. He asked for loyalty and

military service. In return, Yoritomo offered to confirm their land-manager jobs and make those jobs permanent.

After spending twenty years among rural samurai, Yoritomo understood that these fiercely proud men felt like victims. A samurai might manage an aristocrat's estate for decades, collecting rent and taxes from the overworked peasants (while taking a cut for himself as well). Yet the aristocratic landlord in faraway Kyoto could replace him on a whim. Samurai craved job security.

Yoritomo promised it to them. Land ownership would stay the same, he explained, and samurai would still collect rent on behalf of landlords and taxes on behalf of the government. But Yoritomo, not the land-owners, would decide who got the land-manager jobs. Under Yoritomo's new deal, as long as a samurai was loyal to Yoritomo, he couldn't be fired by anybody except Yoritomo. *And* his son could inherit his job. In short, Yoritomo was offering the samurai lifetime employment. Civilian landlords and religious leaders who oversaw land were also given more security. To top it off, Yoritomo allowed his chosen land managers to skim a slightly higher percentage of the profits.

The Chinese character for *samurai* originally meant "to serve a master." Yoritomo intended to alter the meaning a bit. He was going to serve up a bigger slice of Japan's wealth to his loyal men.

Yoritomo knew Taira Kiyomori wanted him dead and would send local Taira allies to kill him. He decided to strike first. Yoritomo didn't ride into battle himself, however. In fact, he always showed a lack of enthusiasm for putting himself in any real danger. Instead, he ordered his father-in-law and their small band of followers to make a surprise nighttime attack on the home of a local Taira administrator. The next morning the Taira's head was delivered to Yoritomo's front porch.

News of severed heads travels fast. Within a week Kiyomori's allies had gathered several thousand troops to hunt down the Minamoto rebels. Yoritomo, his father-in-law, and their three hundred followers retreated into the mountains. They were overtaken in the half-light before dawn. During the melee an arrow pierced Yoritomo's sleeve and lodged harmlessly between the plates of his armor. Beaten and scattered, Yoritomo's forces fled deeper into the rugged terrain. It looked as if Yoritomo's head would soon be on its way to Kyoto.

Many years before, when Yoritomo was a little boy, his nurse had given him a tiny silver statue of Kannon, the Buddhist goddess of mercy. Yoritomo always wore it tied in his topknot. In that desperate hour he pulled it out, explaining to his followers that he might be captured and beheaded. He told them he feared that the Taira might laugh if they found such a babyish thing in his hair.

Yoritomo and his remaining men tried to escape the pursuing Taira. They hoped that the sharp mountain ridges would shield them from the eyes of Taira scouts, but one of the Taira spotted them. This warrior was a calculating fellow named Kagetoki, who had already secretly decided that he liked Yoritomo's new deal. When he returned to the leader of the Taira forces, he said, "There are no traces of anyone on this mountain."

Yoritomo and his men slipped away.

Afterward it seemed as if someone had opened a spigot: eastern samurai flowed steadily from the Taira side to the Minamoto. Yoritomo set up headquarters in Kamakura, a quiet fishing village that was home to a Minamoto family shrine. In Kamakura, Yoritomo welcomed his new vassals (retainers). He accepted almost anyone who pledged their loyalty—even those who had recently been his mortal enemies.

In those days men sometimes inked their names on their arrows in case one was recovered from the body of a high-ranking enemy. Samurai lived for such bragging rights. The arrow that had lodged in Yoritomo's armor during the skirmish in the mountains carried a warrior's name. Knowing full well that the man had almost killed him, Yoritomo pardoned the warrior and allowed him to join the Minamoto ranks.

Perhaps it's not surprising that Yoritomo quickly forgave his former enemies. He needed every samurai he could muster because a Taira army was coming to crush the Minamoto once and for all.

Back in Hiraizumi, Lord Hidehira learned of Yoshitsune's disappearance. He immediately regretted his refusal to let the young man go. Was Yoshitsune not a samurai? How could the boy stay safely in the north while other Minamoto were fighting for their lives? Honor and duty were at stake.

The lord of Hiraizumi summoned two warrior brothers known for bravery and asked them to ride south to join Yoshitsune. Tadanobu was a year or so older than Yoshitsune, and Tsuginobu a year or so younger. They had probably trained with Yoshitsune and knew him well. No doubt Hidehira ordered them to try to keep Yoshitsune alive.

At some point along the road south, Tsuginobu and

Tadanobu overtook Yoshitsune. The trio arrived at Yoritomo's camp only to discover that the fearsome Taira army was already retreating to Kyoto. Whatever disappointment Yoshitsune suffered at arriving a day late, at least he didn't miss the action. The battle of Fuji River was possibly the most anticlimactic "battle" in history.

Kiyomori had expected his army (commanded by one of his grandsons) to quickly squash the Minamoto. The Taira were always a major military power and over the past twenty years had successfully fought pirates and rebellious monks in western Japan. Yet it did not bode well that Kiyomori's strong and competent eldest son had died of illness the year before. And the newest generation of Taira had grown up within Kyoto's silken orbit. In imitation of their social superiors, some of the Taira blackened their teeth (a white smile was considered "wild and barbaric") and powdered their faces. In Kyoto's aristocratic society, mastering poetry was important. Mastering mounted archery wasn't.

In contrast to the well-settled lands around Kyoto, the Minamoto heartland remained a wild place with marshes full of ducks and geese and pasture for raising horses. Minamoto warriors were famous for their toughness and superb riding skills. On his way to war, the Taira commander-in-chief asked a local samurai to describe the Minamoto way of battle. "Once a rider mounts, he never loses his seat; however rugged the terrain he gallops over, his horse never falls," the man claimed. "If he sees his father or son cut down in battle, he rides over the dead body and keeps on fighting."

The Taira army had moved deeper into Minamoto territory. That year only a few days of rain had fallen. Rice and barley withered in the autumn fields; grass crackled and snapped underfoot. As the army advanced eastward, the Taira began to worry. The large number of samurai defecting to Yoritomo shook their confidence. What if they couldn't retreat to Kyoto? What if they were attacked from all sides?

The Taira army had reached the banks of the Fuji River at dusk. Yoritomo's forces waited on the opposite shore. Both sides had set up camp, expecting to clash the following morning. The nervous Taira counted the campfires across the river—so many!—not realizing that many of the fires belonged to peasants who had fled into the hills to escape the battle.

The sky darkened. Without warning, thousands of water birds burst from the marshes near the Taira camp, dark wings whistling in the night.

"The great [Minamoto] force has launched its attack!" the Taira shouted. "We can't hold out if we are surrounded!"

Some warriors seized bows and forgot their arrows, while others picked up quivers but left their bows behind. Men leaped on the wrong horses; some, it is said, "leaped onto tethered beasts and rode in circles around picket stakes." The panicked Taira fled, never realizing that a single Minamoto scout had snuck along the river-bank. The scout had accidentally spooked the birds—as well as the entire Taira army. The Minamoto samurai were probably still laughing the next day when Yoshi-tsune rode into Yoritomo's camp.

Yoshitsune strode to the doorstep of the house where Yoritomo was staying. He announced his name to the guards and asked to speak with his long-lost half brother. Yoritomo's guards apparently thought it was a scam or a joke. They left Yoshitsune standing on the pavement, no doubt seething in anger and embarrassment. Eventually someone told Yoritomo about the stranger planted on his front step. Yoritomo ordered Yoshitsune brought in immediately.

On that autumn day in 1180, the two half brothers could not have been more different. Yoritomo, lord of Kamakura and leader of the Minamoto, had grown up in comfort and security. At fourteen the disaster in Kyoto had shattered his world. He had lost everyone he had ever loved, as well as his home, his status, and his freedom. Twenty years of exile had given him plenty of time to reflect on what had gone wrong. Thirty-four-year-old Minamoto Yoritomo had emerged as a cool politician who avoided risk and understood the value of patience and preparation.

And then there was Yoshitsune.

Yoshitsune hadn't been raised among Minamoto. He had never lived in the Minamoto homeland. He probably didn't look Minamoto—armor details differed by region, and Yoshitsune had been outfitted in the north. He probably didn't sound Minamoto, either. Easterners spoke with harsh accents, but Yoshitsune had spent his entire life in Hiraizumi and the Kyoto area. Virtually everything Yoshitsune knew about being Minamoto had probably come to him secondhand through gossip, stories, and legends. At twenty-one Yoshitsune was a young man of heroic ambitions who was determined to prove himself worthy of a grand legacy. Risk taking was part of his nature.

The meeting between these very different half brothers seems to have been genuinely happy. It is said "the two, recalling the past, wept with joy." Yoritomo generously compared Yoshitsune to the younger brother of Great-Grandfather Yoshiie, who had left the comforts of Kyoto to join Yoshiie in battle against northern barbarians.

After such a favorable reception, Yoshitsune may have hoped for command of Yoritomo's army and an order to pursue and destroy the retreating Taira. If so, he was disappointed. The lord of Kamakura recognized the Taira's vulnerability, but he had more pressing problems. Some eastern samurai still resisted his rule. The yearlong drought had caused the rice harvest to fail, which meant no surplus food to sustain a long cross-country campaign. And Yoritomo may have thought that his enthusiastic younger half brother wasn't quite ready for prime time. The lord of Kamakura would watch . . . and judge.

Back in Kyoto, Taira Kiyomori took the debacle at the Fuji River like a sword in the gut. A few months after the Taira army straggled home, the sixty-four-year-old samurai lord fell ill with a fever. Kiyomori's wife tearfully asked him if he had any last wishes. She expected her husband to request the building of a temple or ask for sacred scriptures to be copied and recited to ease his soul toward its next rebirth.

"Build no halls or pagodas after I die; dedicate no pious works," Kiyomori ordered. "Dispatch the punitive force immediately, decapitate Yoritomo, and hang the head in front of my grave. That will be all the dedication I require."

Kiyomori died two days later. If the old warrior had known what was coming, he'd have demanded Yoshitsune's head, too.

No punitive force of Taira left Kyoto the next year because the harvest failed again. Peasant families abandoned their parched fields and disappeared into the wilderness. Men, women, and children survived on wild berries, nuts, and roots. Those in the capital possessed no such survival skills. When taxes (mostly paid in rice) stopped flowing into Kyoto, city people starved. Weakened by hunger, thousands succumbed to smallpox, measles, or dysentery. Babies and young children were the most vulnerable of all.

"Countless people perished of starvation by the wayside or died next to tile-capped walls," wrote an eyewitness. "Since there was no way to dispose of the bodies, noisome stenches filled the air, and innumerable decomposing corpses shocked the eye. . . . The dead lay so thick in the Kamo riverbed that there was not even room for horses and ox-carriages to pass."

Luckily for the Minamoto, the drought wasn't quite as severe in the eastern part of Japan. Yoritomo used the famine-enforced time-out to consolidate his power. Friendly samurai won plum jobs. Those who opposed the lord of Kamakura lost their livelihood—and sometimes their lives.

Yoritomo's capital grew steadily. Kamakura "had been a secluded place . . . frequented only by fishermen and aged rustics," wrote a source. "But lanes and streets are being laid. . . . The tiled roofs of houses stand in a line." To keep his samurai sharp, Yoritomo organized deer hunts and competitions: archery, ox chasing, and horsemanship. Winners received dyed hides and bolts of dark-blue silk.

During this time another Minamoto half brother arrived in Kamakura. Noriyori was three years older than Yoshitsune. Nothing is known about Noriyori's early life, but his mother's low status (she was an entertainer at an inn) probably caused Kiyomori to overlook him during the hunt for Minamoto heirs. Now Noriyori competed with Yoshitsune for Yoritomo's attention. From what we know about Noriyori, he seems to have been the nail that doesn't stick out and doesn't get hammered down. Not so Yoshitsune.

In 1182 Yoritomo decided to build a new shrine on a hill overlooking Kamakura. The shrine would honor Hachiman, the Shinto god of war and patron god of the Minamoto. At the ceremony marking the raising of the shrine's beams, Yoritomo ordered Yoshitsune to lead out the horses that Yoritomo planned to present as a gift to the shrine's carpenters.

Yoshitsune's pride flared. Was he nothing more than a stable hand? He told Yoritomo that he didn't have any servants available to carry out the order. He clearly didn't intend to lead out the horses himself.

"How can you say such a thing?" demanded Yoritomo. He pointed out that other samurai had performed this humble duty at his request, and without making a fuss.

Yoshitsune stood up apprehensively and took the reins of two horses. Perhaps he realized—too late—that Yoritomo would not forget his disobedience.

That year, 1182, at long last brought rain and a good harvest. And in the ninth month, Yoritomo's wife gave birth to a son. In celebration the lord of Kamakura built a wide avenue that stretched from the beach to the stairs of the family shrine.

The next year, 1183, brought war between the Minamoto and the Taira. Yet Yoritomo's forces weren't the ones doing the fighting.

Yoshitsune, Yoritomo, and Noriyori had a thirty-year-old cousin, Kiso Yoshinaka, who lived in the rugged regions north of Kyoto. Lord Kiso had quickly declared his support for Yoritomo's rebellion. The Taira were anxious to eliminate Kiso, a Minamoto threat looming uncomfortably close to the capital. In early 1183, thousands of Taira samurai rode north. Peasants hid in the forests and fields as the Taira pillaged every food store they could get their hands on along the way. Lord Kiso and his fierce mountain samurai met the Taira in a series of skirmishes and stunned them, winning one fight after another. As spring sprouted into summer, the Taira army was slowly beaten back toward Kyoto.

Retired Emperor Go-Shirakawa saw an opportunity. For too long the imperial family had suffered Taira domination. Despite Go-Shirakawa's unhappy history with Yoshitsune's father, who had kidnapped him and burned his palace, he was willing to ally with another member of the Minamoto family. When one of his ministers suggested aiding Lord Kiso, Go-Shirakawa smiled and replied, "Now is the time to do just that."

Back in Kamakura, Yoritomo fretted. If Kiso captured Kyoto, he would be ideally positioned to control the Retired Emperor and challenge Yoritomo's leadership of the Minamoto. So Yoritomo ordered Kiso to halt his advance south.

But while the lord of Kamakura was sending *Don't*

you dare! messages to Kiso, Retired Emperor Go-Shirakawa was sending Kiso secret missives of the *Do it!* variety. And although Lord Kiso had pledged to obey Yoritomo, he could not resist sweet temptation. In the seventh month of 1183, Kiso Yoshinaka's army advanced toward the outskirts of Kyoto.

After Kiyomori's death, leadership of the Taira had fallen to his feckless son Munemori. Munemori no longer felt safe in Kyoto, where everyone seemed to have turned against the Taira. When he heard about Kiso's advance, he ordered an evacuation to the Taira homeland in western Japan.

In those days thousands of Taira lived in their own suburb just east of Kyoto. They packed as many valuables as possible but couldn't take everything. Refusing to leave anything behind for the detested Minamoto, they torched their abandoned houses, not caring that thousands of nearby commoners' homes also caught fire. Kiyomori's mansion burned at the heart of the immense inferno. Embroidered curtains, lacquered chests, and painted scrolls shot into the air as red flames and fell to earth as black soot. Afterward only a blackened ghost remained of the place where, twenty-three years earlier, Kiyomori had spared a baby named Yoshitsune.

When the Taira made their fiery exit, they took along Emperor Antoku, the six-year-old grandson of both Go-Shirakawa and Kiyomori. They also made off with the Japanese imperial regalia. As everyone knew, the sun goddess had given these ancient treasures—a mirror, a jewel, and a sword—to her grandson, who was the ancestor of the Japanese imperial line. No Japanese emperor could be enthroned without these sacred objects.

Kiyomori's son Munemori attempted to kidnap the

Retired Emperor as well. However, Go-Shirakawa had been through this sort of thing way too many times before. He fled in secret to Kurama, Yoshitsune's boyhood home.

Lord Kiso's forces entered the capital flying the white banners of the Minamoto. The Retired Emperor emerged from hiding. He rewarded Lord Kiso with titles and estates and signed an official edict authorizing him to destroy the Taira. Go-Shirakawa was like a mayor pinning a sheriff's badge on a gunslinger. With a few strokes of ink, Lord Kiso became the government's enforcer and the once-powerful Taira became outlaws.

But Go-Shirakawa quickly regretted his partnership with Kiso. He and the other Kyoto aristocrats had spent two decades secretly despising the "barbaric" Taira, who tried very hard to imitate their social superiors. Now Lord Kiso and his rough mountain warriors gave everyone in Kyoto a taste of *real* barbarism. Kiso's samurai cut green rice for horse fodder, broke into storehouses, robbed merchants, and freely mugged people in the streets. Wayfarers' possessions were seized and the robes stripped from their backs.

This thuggery deepened the misery of a city already maimed by war, famine, disease, and fire. Widespread unrest cut off delivery of the rice that fed the city. "With all the checkpoints closed," says a war chronicle, "those in the provinces could deliver neither official tax goods nor private rents, and people of all degrees in the capital resembled fish in shallow water."

The Retired Emperor sent secret emissaries to Yoritomo asking him to make war on both the Taira *and* Lord Kiso. Go-Shirakawa wanted someone who would act like a sheriff, not an outlaw. In exchange he offered to give Yoritomo official authority to collect all taxes and rent in the east. In other words, Go-Shirakawa would acknowledge the powers that Yoritomo had already seized.

This arrangement appealed to Yoritomo. He didn't want to get rid of the imperial family or the system of titles and land rights that were the foundation of Japanese society. After all, Minamoto status was based on their rank within this tradition. What Yoritomo wanted was power. The imperial family would remain at the center of Japanese religion and ritual; the emperor would still pray for rain, a fertile harvest, and protection from pests. That suited Yoritomo just fine. The lord of Kamakura would advertise himself as "defender of the emperor"— while exerting control behind the scenes.

There was just one problem: Lord Kiso and his men held Kyoto. They wouldn't give up without a fight. Yoritomo needed a general who could lead his troops to victory. Family prestige required Minamoto leadership, so it made sense to appoint either Yoshitsune or Noriyori. Headstrong Yoshitsune clearly wasn't the type to follow orders. On that score Noriyori would be a better choice. Yet submissive men don't make great commanders.

Ever-cautious Yoritomo decided to split his army in two. He gave command of half to Noriyori. The other half went to Yoshitsune.

Yes, Yoshitsune would get his chance to fight the Taira. But first he needed to defeat Lord Kiso quickly and decisively. Any drawn-out conflict that weakened the Minamoto would benefit the Taira. And Yoshitsune needed to outshine his rival half brother, Noriyori.

None of this was going to be easy. Kiso was thirty years old, a successful, battle-tested commander fighting on familiar ground. Twenty-four-year-old Yoshitsune had never been to war and had never led an army. He hadn't set eyes on Kyoto since childhood.

In the first month of 1184, Yoshitsune led three thousand samurai out of Kamakura. He turned west, riding out of the shadows of history and into its full and fatal light.

5

PERILOUS RIVER

KYOTO, 1184

A great gate called Rashōmon framed Kyoto's southern entrance. The structure loomed two stories high, more than one hundred feet wide, and twenty-five feet deep. In the distance, at the end of a wide avenue lined with willow trees, stood the Vermillion Sparrow Gate, which marked the entrance to the imperial palace.

Rashōmon and the six-foot-high ramparts on either side were just for show. The rest of Kyoto was largely unwalled and impossible to defend. The battle for the capital would take place on the city's outskirts.

The armies of Yoshitsune and Noriyori took about three weeks to ride from Kamakura to Kyoto. Since steep mountains protected the capital on the north, east, and west, the best approach was from the south. However, the Minamoto armies would have to cross the fast-flowing Uji River. Noriyori's forces would attempt a crossing at Seta

Bridge, where the waters of Lake Biwa drained into the river. Yoshitsune's forces would try to cross farther south at Uji Bridge.

In the darkness before dawn, Yoshitsune prepared for his first battle. A red brocade under-robe and wide-legged trousers went on first, followed by lacquered iron shin guards and bearskin boots. A servant probably helped him tug on the tight-fitting sleeve armor for his left arm—it had to be snug so it wouldn't catch on his bowstring. One flap of armor was tied under his right arm; a three-sided piece wrapped around the rest of his torso. On that day, it is said, Yoshitsune wore armor with purple lacings. A samurai leader was expected to dress the part—the gaudier the better.

Over his chest a smooth flap of deerskin was pulled tight so Yoshitsune could draw his bow without snagging the edges of his armor plates. A four-paneled armored skirt went around his waist to protect his thighs and hips, and large flaps were rigged to protect his shoulders. He slipped his hands into soft doeskin gloves. Special padding protected his right thumb from the pressure of drawing his bowstring.

Yoshitsune also carried first-class weapons: a sword with gilt-bronze fittings, a rattan-wrapped bow, and a quiver full of arrows fledged with black-and-white eagle feathers. Like most samurai he probably brought along a spare bowstring coiled up in a doughnut-shaped container tied to his waist.

Some warriors disliked helmets and chose not to wear them in battle. As a commander Yoshitsune didn't have that option. Pride demanded that he flaunt his status, so he wore a helmet topped with shiny beetle horns.

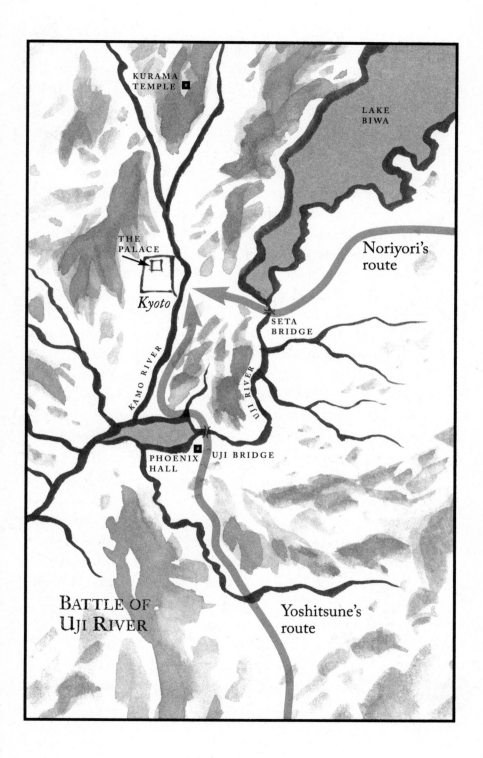

KURAMA
TEMPLE

LAKE
BIWA

THE
PALACE

Kyoto

Noriyori's
route

SETA
BRIDGE

KAMO RIVER

UJI RIVER

PHOENIX
HALL

UJI BRIDGE

BATTLE OF
UJI RIVER

Yoshitsune's
route

Magnificence came at a price, however. Clad in such finery Yoshitsune practically had a bull's-eye painted on his back. Low-ranking warriors in particular salivated at the thought of killing a high-ranking enemy. To die at the hands of an "unworthy" adversary—not just an enemy, but some low-class fellow who couldn't afford glamorous armor—was the nightmare scenario of Yoshitsune and every other high-born samurai.

On that winter morning, as he strapped on his armor and gathered his weapons, was Yoshitsune afraid? Most warriors—even experienced ones—fear death. The possibility of failure may have terrified Yoshitsune even more.

Yoshitsune and his men mounted their warhorses and rode the last stretch to Uji Bridge. His companions from Hiraizumi, the samurai brothers Tadanobu and Tsuginobu, probably rode at his side. The army gathered on the southern bank of the Uji River. Nearby stood the graceful Phoenix Hall, where Yoshitsune's elderly relative, the warrior-poet Minamoto Yorimasa, had killed himself in the face of defeat. Dawn was just breaking. Through dim light and soft fog, Yoshitsune looked for Uji Bridge.

The bridge was gone; Lord Kiso's men had torn it to pieces. On the opposite bank the defenders had driven stakes into the shallows, stretched ropes between them, and constructed floating barricades bristling with sharp branches. Between the two armies roared a furious river 170 yards wide. Icy snowmelt smashed against boulders, twisted into whirlpools, and crested into waves. The Uji was ready to swallow samurai.

What to do?

Yoshitsune's options were already limited. He commanded about three thousand men, but his army was not a well-organized force. It was nothing but a large and loose assembly of samurai squads. Each squad—numbering about six to twenty men—was the kind of group Yoshitsune had trained with in Hiraizumi: a tight-knit band of family, friends, and close retainers. Samurai bands specialized in highly mobile, hit-and-run tactics designed for raiding neighbors or chasing bandits across Japan's mountainous landscape. Large-scale, coordinated maneuvers simply weren't part of their playbook. In fact, if history's great fighters were gathered together, Yoshitsune's men would find a lot more in common with fiercely independent Comanches than disciplined Roman legionnaires.

Yoshitsune also had to deal with the samurai desire for personal glory. Everybody wanted bragging rights, whether for being the first to attack or for killing a high-ranking enemy. Controlling an uncoordinated army of showboats was a general's nightmare. Unless . . .

Yoshitsune watched the icy waters rushing past. "What shall we do?" he asked his men. "Would it be best to go around . . . ? Shall we wait for the river to subside?"

Samurai generals did not usually consult their troops in such an open and casual manner. Yoshitsune's men felt flattered.

"It is not some unknown body of water that has suddenly materialized: it is the outlet of Lake Biwa, and it will not go down, no matter how long we wait," a warrior explained. "Nobody can bridge it for you, either."

"I'll test it for you!" cried another.

This offer was apparently what Yoshitsune was hoping for. A samurai wearing heavy armor enjoyed a good dunking about as much as a cat, but a competitive spirit suddenly washed caution away. Within minutes five hundred warriors lined the water's edge, bridle to bridle, their horses breathing steam into the frosty air. Each man hoped to seize the honor of being the first across the Uji River. But by sending his samurai into the river, Yoshitsune was taking an enormous risk. At the moment his force outnumbered Lord Kiso's defenders. How many would survive the crossing?

Yoshitsune and his men drove their heels into their horses' flanks. They plunged down the steep banks and crashed into the frigid water.

One brawny stallion surged into the lead. Yoritomo had loaned his magnificent warhorse Ikezuki ("Bad-Tempered Biter") to a favored retainer. The samurai clung to the saddle as Ikezuki fought his way, wild-eyed, across the roaring river. They had almost reached the opposite bank when Ikezuki faltered. His rider, realizing that Lord Kiso's men had strung trip lines underwater, drew his sword and slashed the hidden ropes. Ikezuki barreled through the barricade and heaved onto the riverbank, winning his rider immortality as "first man across the Uji."

Kiso Yoshinaka's men unleashed a storm of arrows at Yoshitsune and the other samurai still struggling through the roiling waters. One warrior's horse was struck in the forehead by an arrow. Undaunted, the man used his bow as a staff to ford the final stretch of water. Upon reaching the other side, he mounted a loose horse and promptly killed a kinsman of Lord Kiso's.

More Minamoto struggled ashore. They galloped their horses among the enemy, firing a barrage of arrows. The assault shocked and demoralized Lord Kiso's troops. They had counted on the river and their barricade for protection and had never really expected to fight. After putting up meager resistance, they broke and fled.

Yoshitsune didn't even wait for the battle to end. He called a handful of men to his side and—no doubt still dripping—galloped his warhorse toward Kyoto.

In 1160 Yoshitsune's father had ridden to a palace in search of Retired Emperor Go-Shirakawa. Twenty-four years later, almost to the day, Yoshitsune did the same.

The two-pronged assault by Yoshitsune and Noriyori had forced their cousin Lord Kiso to split his army. In addition, a former ally of Kiso's had suddenly decided to support Yoritomo. Lord Kiso divided his forces three ways to counter the three separate threats. After six months of being grand master of Kyoto, Kiso's sudden change in fortune seemed to unnerve him. Instead of leading at least one of the three parts of his army, he lingered at his residence in Kyoto. If things went badly, Kiso had the usual samurai backup plan: kidnap the Retired Emperor.

Messengers brought news of Yoshitsune's startlingly quick advance. Alarmed, Kiso decided to flee without stopping to grab Go-Shirakawa. Several hundred of his retainers rode east with him. Their job was to save their lord from enemy headhunters. Unfortunately for Kiso, Noriyori's men had managed to cross the river at Seta Bridge and defeat Kiso's defenders. Now they were spreading out to hunt down Kiso's surviving troops.

Noriyori's samurai had no trouble spotting Lord Kiso—he sat on a gold-edged saddle and wore a horned helmet and a red brocade robe under armor laced with patterned silk. His flashy armor broadcast TROPHY HEAD to anyone within sight. Kiso and his retainers were forced to fight a series of desperate running battles. Like offensive linemen guarding their quarterback, Lord Kiso's men were supposed to protect their leader—especially his blind side. Mounted samurai wanted to approach their enemy from behind and on the right, because it is easy for a right-handed archer to swing toward targets on the left, but much more difficult to twist in the other direction. Lord Kiso's samurai did their job—but at a cost. After each skirmish fewer were left alive.

The shadows lengthened and the winter air grew colder. Both men and horses were at their limits when yet another squad of warriors spotted Kiso and gave chase. A thin film of ice had formed across a sodden rice paddy, and Lord Kiso, mistaking it for solid ground, galloped his warhorse straight into it. The stallion sank up to its ears in the mire. Kiso threw a glance over his shoulder—and an arrow plunged into his face.

His head was taken back to the capital and hung from a tree beside the Kyoto prison gate.

A cloud of dust crowned by white Minamoto banners moved through the streets of Kyoto. When the horsemen reached the Retired Emperor's palace, his guards assumed that the banners belonged to Lord Kiso. They barred the entrance.

Yoshitsune yelled that he was the younger brother of Yoritomo, "arrived from the east at your service! Be kind enough to open the gate!"

Later it was said that the Retired Emperor was delighted to see Yoshitsune. Perhaps he was. But Go-Shirakawa certainly hadn't forgotten that twenty-four years earlier

Yoshitsune's father had set fire to one of his palaces and murdered everyone in it. Nor had he forgotten that Yoshitsune's cousin Lord Kiso had recently plundered his capital or that Yoshitsune's half brother Yoritomo had illegally seized power in the east.

For his part Yoshitsune certainly wanted to protect the Retired Emperor from Lord Kiso. But his swift ride to the capital may have had another motivation: to make sure he, and not Noriyori, got credit for coming to Go-Shirakawa's aid. Victory is sweet. Victory in a sibling rivalry is even sweeter.

Yoshitsune didn't enjoy his triumph for very long. In fact, he barely had time to dry out his armor. Just nine days after crossing the Uji River, Yoshitsune and his samurai rode to war once again.

Thousands of Minamoto warriors flowed out of the capital along the road heading southwest toward the Taira homeland. Most commoners probably stayed out of sight, since samurai had a habit of kidnapping people and forcing them to work in the army as servants. Yet despite warnings from their parents, some children probably watched the parade. How often did a country child see fluttering white banners, sleek horses with red silk bridles, and men wearing armor that made them resemble monstrous, hard-shelled beetles? After the show ended, perhaps some of the children grabbed sticks and fought their own imaginary battles.

Yoshitsune was a man who might sympathize. Not so long ago he, too, had dreamed of becoming a samurai. The temple boy had left his play swords behind, but his desire remained the same: to take revenge on the Taira.

6

MIDNIGHT STRIKE

ICHI-NO-TANI, 1184

The Taira had not been idle. While Lord Kiso was enjoying his six-month free-for-all in Kyoto, the Taira were fortifying a narrow strip of land on the Settsu coast. They chose a spot flanked by steep mountains to the north and sea to the south. On the eastern side, where a shallow river crossed the beach and emptied into the ocean, they built Ikuta-no-Mori, a barricade of felled trees. On the western edge they erected a fortress called Ichi-no-Tani, set against steep cliffs. They dug ditches and constructed palisades; inside Ichi-no-Tani's wooden walls rose storerooms, stables, barracks, and archers' towers.

The Taira built Ikuta-no-Mori and Ichi-no-Tani because they didn't want to fight the Minamoto on open ground. The Taira had fine reputations as sailors who controlled the sea trade throughout western Japan. But the

Minamoto were better horsemen. The Taira knew that Minamoto samurai could ride circles around lesser riders and decimate anyone fighting on foot. So the Taira decided to neutralize the Minamoto's biggest advantage by raining a storm of arrows on their enemies from behind barricades and palisades. Against such fortresses the mobility of the Minamoto horsemen would count for nothing. And even if the Taira couldn't hold the Minamoto at the Ikuta-no-Mori barricade, they could fall back to unconquerable Ichi-no-Tani.

The Taira didn't even need a clear-cut victory. Just keeping their foothold on the Settsu coast would curb the Minamoto and count as a Taira win. Best of all, their ships anchored offshore offered the ultimate security for their most important assets: Emperor Antoku and the imperial regalia. The Minamoto didn't have a navy.

To defend these positions, the Taira amassed twenty thousand fighters. The entire Minamoto army numbered no more than seven thousand.

Yoshitsune and Noriyori left Kyoto separately. Noriyori led his forces—three to four thousand men—along the shorter coastal route. He would attack Ikuta-no-Mori from the east. Yoshitsune and his men, numbering about three thousand, followed the longer, rougher route across the mountains to the north. After crossing the mountains his warriors would then circle around and attack Ichi-no-Tani from the west.

Yoshitsune rode out of Kyoto on a horse named Tayūguro ("Black Captain"). Tayūguro had been given to him, along with a gold-edged saddle, by Retired Emperor

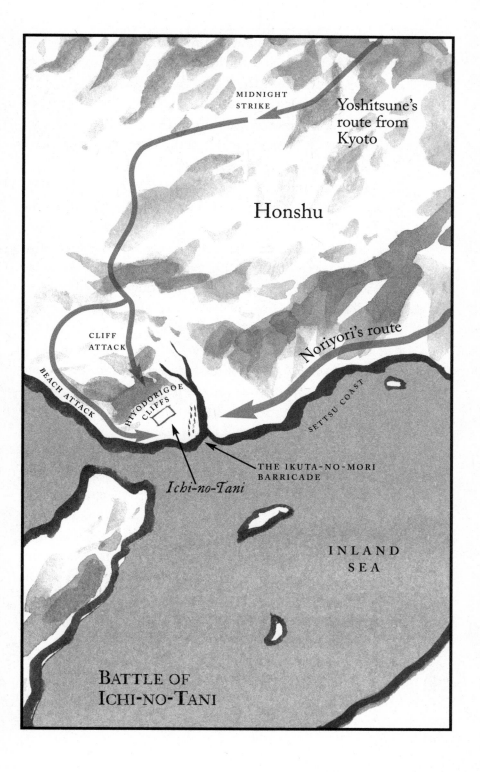

MIDNIGHT
STRIKE

Yoshitsune's
route from
Kyoto

Honshu

CLIFF
ATTACK

Noriyori's route

BEACH ATTACK

HIYODORIGOE
CLIFFS

SETTSU COAST

THE IKUTA-NO-MORI
BARRICADE

Ichi-no-Tani

INLAND
SEA

BATTLE OF
ICHI-NO-TANI

Go-Shirakawa. During their meeting the Retired Emperor had emphasized the importance of recovering the imperial regalia from the Taira. As long as the Taira held the mirror, jewel, and sword, it would be difficult to appoint a new emperor. If Go-Shirakawa also expressed concern about his kidnapped grandson, little Emperor Antoku, the war chronicle doesn't mention it.

The imperial gift of horse and saddle probably meant a great deal to Yoshitsune. In Hiraizumi he had relied on his foster father's charity and in Kamakura on Yoritomo's. But now the Retired Emperor favored him. Yoshitsune had every reason to hope for even greater rewards—if he could defeat the Taira and recapture the imperial regalia.

Heroes always seem to need sidekicks to help with their quests. By the time Yoshitsune rode to war against the Taira, he had attracted a very unusual group of companions. Every high-ranking samurai, of course, wanted close retainers who would act as bodyguards. Yet training and equipping your own team of samurai was like owning a professional sports franchise: an expensive proposition.

Yoshitsune wasn't wealthy. But the motley crew that formed around him didn't seem to care. His closest friends included Tsuginobu and Tadanobu, the brothers from Hiraizumi. Because of their northern roots, they were probably considered barbarians by the Minamoto samurai. (A "barbarian" was anybody who lived farther away from Kyoto than you did.) A man named Ise Saburō also rode with Yoshitsune. Ise Saburō's enemies claimed he had once been a mountain bandit—a charge he did not deny.

By the time Yoshitsune rode for Ichi-no-Tani (and possibly earlier) he had also made friends with a warrior-monk named Benkei. In those days some of the larger temples employed monks with martial training as private security forces. According to legend Benkei was a ferocious fighter, but so wild and boisterous that no temple wanted him. Yoshitsune did.

Maybe Yoshitsune's humble upbringing at Kurama had something to do with it, or perhaps it was the time he spent disguised as the gold merchant's servant. And Yoshitsune had always been an outsider, whether at Kurama, Hiraizumi, or Kamakura. Maybe he was drawn to others on the fringes. Whatever the reasons, he seemed most comfortable with his outcast band of warriors. The bond between Yoshitsune, Benkei, Tsuginobu, Tadanobu, and Ise Saburō would last for the rest of their lives.

Yoshitsune, his companions, and his three thousand warriors headed toward the Settsu coast, weaving their way through mountain pines and cold gray stones. Six days after leaving Kyoto, Yoshitsune's scouts spotted an advance force of several thousand Taira camped about nine miles away. The winter sky was already dark. Plunge ahead? Or wait until morning?

Just as at Uji River, Yoshitsune asked for advice. A warrior pointed out that more Taira might be arriving the next day. It would be better to ride through the darkness and surprise the Taira with a night attack right now, while the Minamoto still outnumbered their enemies. This wasn't considered treachery, because samurai didn't worry about "fighting fair." In Yoshitsune's world, night raids, sneak attacks, deception, and shooting someone in the back were all acceptable tactics. Only a fool let his guard down.

Yoshitsune knew that a midnight attack would be difficult and dangerous—so naturally he loved the idea.

When someone pointed out that they wouldn't be able to see where they were going, Yoshitsune ordered his men to set fire to trees, fields, and commoners' houses along the way.

For a warrior Yoshitsune was unusually civilized in his dealings with common people. He made sure that his warriors behaved well in Kyoto—no thievery or bullying happened on his watch. Yet he remained a samurai. Samurai didn't see themselves as protectors of the common people; a peasant had no more "rights" than an ox. So the fires were lit. Yoshitsune and his men rode nine miles "in light as bright as day," their way illuminated by the misery of others.

The Taira had also scouted the Minamoto position. However, the Taira leaders assumed the Minamoto would do what they did: make camp at nightfall and get a good night's rest before the next day's battle. Though some in the front lines stayed alert, "the ones in the rear stretched out and went to sleep, their heads pillowed on helmets, armor-sleeves, and quivers."

Battle cries and the thump of galloping hooves woke the Taira. Warriors snatched weapons and desperately tried to dodge the onrushing horsemen and whistling arrows, but hundreds died in the midnight melee. The survivors fled south under the cover of darkness to Ichi-no-Tani and Ikuta-no-Mori.

Yoshitsune's bold strike proved that the battle of Uji River was no fluke. He was a gifted leader. However, the night assault was exactly the sort of hit-and-run, circle-and-shoot skirmish that played to the strengths of Minamoto horsemen. What could Yoshitsune do against the towers of Ichi-no-Tani?

On the other side of the mountain range, Noriyori's army had already reached Ikuta-no-Mori. The Minamoto planted their white banners and made camp just out of bow shot across the shallow river that ran between them and the Taira barricade. As the Taira watched from behind their piles of trees and branches, Noriyori's men calmly fed their horses and cooked their dinner. Did the Minamoto make loud jokes about the "battle" of Fuji River and the Taira fleeing at the first quack of a duck?

Noriyori's men didn't attack that night; they didn't armor up the next day, either. Noriyori was waiting for Yoshitsune. According to their pre-arranged plan, Noriyori's and Yoshitsune's armies would stage a simultaneous attack the following morning. But their strategy would fail if Yoshitsune couldn't get through the mountains.

The morning after his successful midnight strike, Yoshitsune split his forces. He sent the bulk of his three thousand men off with a sub-commander. He ordered them to follow the ravines leading southwest. When his army reached the sea, they would ride around the headland and attack Ichi-no-Tani from the front. Yoshitsune and a band of thirty warriors would strike from a different direction.

The steep slopes rising behind Ichi-no-Tani were called the Hiyodorigoe Cliffs. The Taira considered Ichi-no-Tani impregnable from that direction. Yoshitsune did not. There was only one problem: Yoshitsune had never seen the Hiyodorigoe Cliffs, and neither had anyone under his command. They knew the cliffs lay somewhere to the south, but they needed to find just the right spot directly above Ichi-no-Tani.

One of Yoshitsune's men suggested tossing the reins over an old horse's neck and driving it ahead in the hopes that the beast would sense the best path down. "Excellent advice," Yoshitsune agreed.

They chose an old white horse and followed it all day. Sometimes their path climbed toward the clouds; sometimes they descended into thickly wooded ravines where snow bunched on the pine trees. Snowflakes drifted past their faces. Yet still they could not find the cliffs. As the sun faded they stopped to rest while Benkei went off in search of help. He returned with an old hunter and the hunter's son, an eighteen-year-old named Washinoo.

Yoshitsune asked the old man if they could descend to Ichi-no-Tani from the cliffs. The old hunter declared it impossible. Yoshitsune persisted: Did deer ever go down that way?

The man admitted that they did.

"Why, it sounds like a regular racetrack!" Yoshitsune said. "A horse can certainly go where a deer goes."

This was obviously not true, but nobody contradicted Yoshitsune. The hunter—apparently appalled at such insanity—hastily claimed he was too feeble to help. He offered his son instead.

Yoshitsune and his friends decided Washinoo would not only become their new guide—he would become their new mascot. They tied his hair up, samurai style.

In later centuries samurai status would be jealously guarded and limited to those born into the samurai class. In Yoshitsune's time, however, a "samurai" was more loosely defined. Anybody who could afford the gear and the training could be a warrior. As someone who hunted for a living, Washinoo was probably already an excellent archer. If Yoshitsune gave the teenager a horse and armor and made him part of his band, then Washinoo was a samurai. More or less.

It seems Washinoo didn't mind being kidnapped by lunatics. He remained with Yoshitsune until the very end.

Yoshitsune's band made camp. Possibly the men slept for a few hours. Before dawn, amid a kitten-soft snowfall, the samurai mounted their horses. Washinoo guided them through ravines and over ridges to the top of the Hiyodorigoe Cliffs, where the ground dropped off into ominous blackness. Yoshitsune and his warriors settled in to wait for first light.

In the quiet before dawn, it is said, the silvery notes of a flute drifted from the fortress.

The morning sun lit the wooden walls of Ichi-no-Tani. It spread down the beach and across the water, where a line of Taira vessels bobbed at anchor. The wives and children of high-ranking Taira waited on the ships, along with little Emperor Antoku and the imperial regalia.

Daylight fingertipped its way across the rough brown sand. Armored bowmen took their stances on the archery platforms; rows of saddled horses waited inside the fortress. Once the Minamoto had dashed themselves to death against the walls, and their ranks were fatally thinned by the archers on the towers, the Taira planned to ride out and finish off their enemies. Maybe Yoritomo's head wasn't yet available for the soothing of Taira Kiyomori's spirit, but the heads of Noriyori and Yoshitsune would do nicely.

The war chronicle says, "The full-drawn bows were like half-moons at the warriors' breasts; the glittering three-foot swords resembled streaks of autumn frost crossing their hips. The countless red banners unfurled on the heights danced like leaping flames in the spring breeze."

While waiting to attack Ichi-no-Tani from the front, a Minamoto father fussed over his sixteen-year-old son. "Keep pushing your armor up," he reminded the boy. "Don't let an arrow through. See that your neck-guard is low. Don't get shot in the face."

Up on the Hiyodorigoe Cliffs, Yoshitsune and his men finally understood what they had gotten themselves into. Their perch offered a lovely view of the sea and the long ribbon of beach stretching down to the Taira and Minamoto forces massed at Ikuta-no-Mori. Directly below, perhaps just visible, stood Ichi-no-Tani. The cliffs tilted sharply down in front of them, a morass of scraggly trees with knobby roots like trip wires, crosscut with ravines and banks—often hidden by shrubs—that might drop six, seven, or twenty feet. It was enough to give even a deer vertigo.

On this tense and slippery spot, Yoshitsune and his friends waited.

Shortly after daybreak Noriyori's riders splashed across the shallow river and charged the barricade at Ikuta-no-Mori. The bulk of Yoshitsune's army had arrived at the coast in the middle of the night; taking their cue from Noriyori's attack, they rounded the headland and galloped toward Ichi-no-Tani.

"Their shouts and yells awoke echoes in the mountains; the hoofbeats of their galloping horses reverberated like thunder; the arrows they exchanged resembled falling rain," says the war chronicle.

The sounds of war drums and battle cries drifted up

the Hiyodorigoe Cliffs. Yoshitsune and his band mounted their horses.

"All right, take them down! Do as I do!" Yoshitsune called. Digging his heels into Tayūguro's dark flanks, he plunged over the edge.

7

HOOVES LIKE HAILSTONES

Ichi-no-Tani, 1184

Down below, Yoshitsune's men were dying. Hillocks of dead horses and men piled up under the archery platforms. The war chronicle says, "The fierce combat caused the mountains to reverberate and the ground to tremble. And despite the efforts of the men from Kamakura, an easy victory was not in sight, for the castle walls towered high on the boulders which could not be negotiated by the horses, and the deepness of the ravine cut off penetration."

The Minamoto at Ikuta-no-Mori fared no better. They could not break through the fiercely defended barricade. Taira arrows felled both men and horses; the dead and wounded littered the beach and the river shallows.

Everything depended on Yoshitsune.

He and his warriors slipped and slid down the cliffs, urging their mounts with yells of "Ei! Ei!" The horsemen leaned back as far as possible, heads almost touching their horses' tails, desperate to keep from tumbling head over heels. The angle was so steep that the stirrup-edges of riders behind almost touched the helmets of the men just ahead. Many brave samurai rode, it is said, with their eyes closed.

Clattering, grunting, they fell into the enemy camp, thudding onto the low roofs of sleeping quarters built against the cliff face. One final plummet by their sturdy stallions sent them to the ground inside Ichi-no-Tani. Yoshitsune's men pulled torches from their saddlebags and lit them. Sparks flying, they galloped through the fortress, torching buildings and piles of horse fodder— anything that might burn. A violent sea wind hurled the blaze from structure to structure. The Taira archers raining death on the army outside the walls turned in astonishment to see dark silhouettes menacing their lines from within, backed by a wall of smoke and flame.

The Taira panicked. Archers abandoned the towers, threw open Ichi-no-Tani's gates, and leaped onto their horses. Those on foot grabbed swords, *naginata* (spears with curved blades), or *kumade* (shafts fitted with iron claws). The battle spilled out and spread across the beach. Groups of Minamoto and Taira horsemen swooped and circled, releasing their arrows at close range, aiming at fatal gaps in their opponents' armor. A raised arm, a turned head, or a shifted leg—arrows pierced armpits, necks, and knees. Men on foot were at a great disadvantage. Those with naginata protected themselves by slashing at horses and riders, while those armed with kumade used the weapon's iron claw to drag enemy horsemen to the trampled ground. Warriors who had exhausted their arrows wrestled each other out of the saddle and finished their fight with swords or daggers. The bamboo grass lining the beach reddened with blood.

The Taira commander at Ichi-no-Tani was Kiyomori's brother. He rode out of the flaming fortress surrounded by one hundred riders—all recently recruited from nearby provinces. When confronted with a determined band of Minamoto, the commander's escorts abandoned him.

The commander put up a good fight. One of the Minamoto managed to pull him off his horse, but the Taira commander pinned the Minamoto to the sand. As the Taira raised his dagger for the kill, another Minamoto rode up and sliced off his arm. The dying Taira tried to recite his final invocations to Buddha, but an impatient Minamoto slashed off his head mid-prayer.

Down the beach at Ikuta-no-Mori, Noriyori's forces were still struggling to break through the Taira barricade. But when the Taira saw smoke and flames rising from Ichi-no-Tani, they realized they had lost their fallback position. The Ikuta-no-Mori commander—one of Kiyomori's sons—ordered a retreat to the Taira ships waiting offshore. Morale and discipline vanished. As the Taira abandoned their positions, the Minamoto horsemen broke through the barricade. Now, on the open ground of the beach, the Minamoto could do what they did best: ride circles around their enemies and shoot them down.

The Ikuta-no-Mori commander, along with his son and a retainer, galloped his stallion toward the rescue boats. A group of Minamoto gave chase and felled the retainer with an arrow to the neck. The commander's son died, too. The commander escaped by driving his horse—a magnificent black stallion—into the sea. The warhorse swam nearly a mile before reaching one of the Taira ships. There was not enough room on the vessel for the horse, so after the commander was pulled out of the water, the horse was left behind to fend for itself. As the vessel set sail, the stallion swam forlornly in the wake.

A Taira samurai notched an arrow and aimed, saying, "He will fall into enemy hands. I'll kill him."

"It makes no difference who gets him," the Ikuta-no-Mori commander protested. "He saved my life. Don't shoot."

Still the horse refused to turn for shore. He continued swimming, gradually falling farther and farther behind the Taira ship. At last the stallion gave up and returned to the beach. But he stood looking out to sea, dripping and anxious, neighing all the while.

Several Taira boats had been left near the water's edge. As scores of samurai scrambled desperately aboard, three of the heavily overweighted vessels sank. Taira leaders quickly decided that only "men of quality" would be allowed on the ships. Low-ranking samurai who tried to climb aboard by clutching the sides of the vessels had their arms slashed off, "and they ended as rows of corpses, reddening the water's edge at Ichi-no-Tani."

A Minamoto warrior rode along the beach scouting for the sort of head that would bring him honor and a hefty reward. He spotted a Taira riding through the shallows toward a waiting boat. The Taira wore resplendent green-laced armor, a horned helmet, and a gilt-fitted scabbard—sure signs of a high-ranking warrior. He might even be a member of Kiyomori's family. The Minamoto hungered for such a trophy.

He yelled to the Taira, "It is dishonorable to show your back to an enemy. Return!"

The Taira could have ignored the taunt and escaped. Yet pride turned him around.

The Minamoto charged, tackling the Taira right off

his horse. The two crashed to the sand. The Minamoto samurai tore off the Taira's horned helmet, raised his dagger—and froze.

A teenage boy stared up at him. Like other Taira of his generation, he had been raised in Kyoto and had the lightly powdered face and blackened teeth of an aristocrat. He didn't look like a warrior at all.

The Taira boy, whose name was Atsumori, didn't beg for mercy. He might not have been a hardened warrior, but he was samurai enough to know his fate. Although Atsumori was Kiyomori's nephew, he refused to tell the Minamoto who he was, saying only, "I am a desirable opponent for you. Ask about me after you take my head."

The Minamoto warrior hesitated. The boy was no older than his own son. He desperately wanted to spare him, but when he looked around, he saw other Minamoto approaching. One was a hard-eyed man named Kagetoki.

Kagetoki was the samurai who had saved Yoritomo's life when Yoritomo was hiding in the mountains at the very beginning of the Minamoto rebellion. After betraying his Taira lord and joining the Minamoto, Kagetoki had become Yoritomo's most trusted vassal. Other warriors found Kagetoki self-centered and contemptuous of anyone he outranked—and he outranked almost everybody. There was no question that Kagetoki would kill the young Taira. Gleefully.

The Minamoto warrior promised Atsumori he would offer prayers for the soothing of the boy's soul. Then, weeping, he killed the youth and sliced off his head. Afterward he found a flute in a brocade bag tied to the boy's side. The Minamoto sorrowfully recalled the flute music that had drifted from Ichi-no-Tani in the darkness before dawn.

Yes, the samurai wept. But his blade still fell.

The fighting continued for about an hour. Taira who reached the safety of their ships sailed out of reach; those left behind either died or escaped into the mountains. As Ichi-no-Tani continued to burn, the Minamoto rounded up prisoners and examined bodies. Several thousand Taira had been killed. The list of the dead included one of Taira Kiyomori's brothers, five of his nephews, two of his sons, and two of his grandsons. The Minamoto gathered the most important heads for display. One week later each head was labeled with a red tag and tied to a tree near the Kyoto prison. One of the rotting heads belonged to Atsumori, the boy who had so valiantly turned to face his Minamoto foe.

Those wounded at Ichi-no-Tani, Minamoto and Taira alike, suffered brutally. In twelfth-century Japan there were no painkillers, no antibiotics, and no surgery. Stitches were unknown. Lightly wounded men wrapped cloth around gashes and gritted their teeth. Severely wounded men died. But many more of those dead men were Taira; the Minamoto losses were relatively minor. Much of the credit went to Yoshitsune, who had broken the back of the Taira defenses and broken their will as well.

Ichi-no-Tani made Yoshitsune a samurai rock star. From that day on, people would speak of him in the same breathless way they spoke of his great-grandfather Yoshiie, the barbarian killer, and his uncle Tametomo, the famous archer and inventor of seppuku. At Uji River, during the midnight strike in the mountains, and at Ichi-no-Tani, Yoshitsune had demonstrated his brilliance as a commander. He knew his men, he could read his opponents, and he understood how to use the hit-and-run tactics of a small samurai band to control the outcome of a larger conflict.

But Yoshitsune wasn't finished. The Taira leader—Kiyomori's son Munemori—had escaped. The Taira still owned a fleet of ships. They still controlled all of western Japan. And they still had Emperor Antoku and the imperial regalia. The Taira wouldn't give up any of those things without a fight.

8

INTO THE STORM

The genius of the Japanese sword lies in its structure. The blade is made from two kinds of steel: a rigid steel that holds the sharp edge and does the cutting, and a flexible steel that forms the backbone. When forged into one blade, these sibling steels produce a sword that can slice without snapping.

Similarly, the partnership forged between the brilliant general Yoshitsune and the brilliant politician Yoritomo seemed ideal. Yet within six months pride and jealousy would fracture the brothers' relationship—and almost derail the campaign against the Taira.

Yoshitsune returned to Kyoto after his victory at Ichi-no-Tani. Immediate pursuit wasn't an option. The Taira had sailed west into lands bordering the Inland Sea. To mount a campaign against them, the Minamoto needed allies with ships.

Yoritomo laid the groundwork. The lord of Kamakura sent trusted vassals into the west to offer samurai lords his seductive new deal: permanent land-management jobs in exchange for loyalty and military service. He also sent a series of "requests" to Go-Shirakawa, asking the Retired Emperor to formally recognize his military authority over eastern Japan and extend that authority to western Japan as well. Go-Shirakawa wasn't in a position to refuse. Most samurai used swords and arrows to take what they wanted, but Yoritomo also conquered with ink and paper.

Significantly, Yoritomo also insisted that the Retired Emperor not award titles to any samurai without prior approval from Kamakura. Yoritomo wanted all samurai competing for *his* favor, not the Retired Emperor's. That included Yoshitsune.

After Ichi-no-Tani, Yoritomo made Yoshitsune his chief deputy in Kyoto. Yoshitsune was suddenly thrust into the heart of the aristocratic world that had awed and intimidated the samurai for centuries.

Post-famine, post-war Kyoto was full of beggars, ruined houses, and filthy ditches. Yet behind the tile-roofed walls of their compounds, the families of the elite enjoyed graceful mansions set in idyllic gardens filled with artificial streams and lakes, horse-racing tracks, dance stages, and fishing pavilions. Within this rarified world a nobleman or noblewoman's reputation hinged on his or her ability to compose soulful poetry inked with an elegant hand. Even casual notes between friends were written in poetic style. Attention was lavished on the shade and scent of the paper, the fresh flower tied to the note, and the dress of the servant who delivered it. In this refined society, the poet's status was further enhanced if each of these elements subtly expressed a poignant appreciation of the passing of time and a deep sensitivity to nature.

In Yoshitsune's world, status involved severed heads.

The young hero was probably an object of curiosity to the aristocratic women who peeked from behind half-raised bamboo curtains arranged to hide their faces but not their glorious clothes. A lady might layer twenty silk robes to create multiple lines of color at her sleeve and hem, and top it all with an exquisite over-robe: lavender dotted with plum blossoms, perhaps, or white embroidered with birds and butterflies. To walk in this costume was like dragging around several sets of bedding—comforters included.

However intriguing Yoshitsune might have been, the noblewomen probably didn't find him handsome. Aristocrats blackened their teeth. Yoshitsune had a scary white smile.

Yoshitsune wasn't lonely, however. Sometime during his stay in Kyoto, he met eighteen-year-old Shizuka, the most famous entertainer in Japan. *Shirabyōshi* ("white rhythm") were dancers who dressed in men's white over-shirts and sang popular songs while pounding out a beat on handheld drums. Twelfth-century Japanese men found this wildly sexy.

Storytellers claimed that when the terrible drought gripped the country, Retired Emperor Go-Shirakawa asked one hundred monks to pray for rain. The sky remained clear. Next the desperate Retired Emperor invited one hundred dancers to try their luck. Ninety-nine failed. Yet when Shizuka danced, "lightning flashed, and the capital was

pelted by a drenching rain which continued for three days."
The ex-emperor announced that Shizuka had saved the
state and officially named her the best dancer in Japan.

Yoshitsune first glimpsed Shizuka, it is said, as she
danced beside a pond at an aristocrat's lavish party. Shortly
afterward the superstar samurai and the superstar dancer
became lovers.

Early 1184 warmed into spring. As the cherry trees began
to bloom, Minamoto spies reported that the Taira had settled on Yashima, an island in the Inland Sea.

Yoritomo sent his right-hand man—the arrogant and
much-disliked Kagetoki—into the west to secure more
boats. Yoshitsune expected to lead the Minamoto army
into the field that fall. Timing was important: the Minamoto needed to sail to Yashima before winter storms
made the seas too dangerous.

While waiting for his fleet to assemble, Yoshitsune
kept busy. Some samurai had used the civil war as an
excuse to settle old scores and seize land belonging to
temples, so Yoshitsune sent men into the countryside to
establish law and order. He may have reunited with his
mother, Tokiwa—or he may have avoided her because she
had borne Kiyomori a daughter. No doubt a meeting between Yoshitsune and a Taira half sister would have been
more than a little awkward.

In the wake of the Minamoto triumph, everyone
knew that Yoritomo would "request" that the Retired Emperor award titles to the commanders who had distin-
guished themselves in the recent battles. Yoshitsune, the

man most responsible for victory at the Uji River and Ichi-no-Tani, had every reason to expect the highest honors. And Yoshitsune probably craved recognition more than anyone. He had lived most of his life without it.

In midsummer, word finally arrived from Kamakura. Half brother Noriyori would become a provincial governor. A governorship gave him the right to collect rice taxes and also skim a generous amount for himself. Noriyori didn't even have to live in his new province—he could assign the actual work to somebody else while reaping the financial rewards. On top of that, Noriyori would receive a court title, bumping him into the Japanese nobility. Several Minamoto subcommanders also received governorships.

Yoshitsune got nothing.

It is easy to imagine Yoshitsune's shock and anger. He had led the Minamoto to victory against both Lord Kiso and the Taira and redeemed Minamoto honor. What had he done to deserve such humiliation? He was Yoritomo's representative in Kyoto—how could he do his job, in a world where rank was everything, without a court title? A man needed to be fifth rank or higher just to enter certain parts of the imperial palace.

Yoritomo's reasons for snubbing Yoshitsune can only be guessed. Yoshitsune wasn't just another retainer—he could claim leadership of the Minamoto if anything happened to Yoritomo. Yoritomo probably felt threatened by his younger half brother's popularity. Yoshitsune was a war hero and well liked by many at the imperial court. The Retired Emperor favored him; his warriors loved him. The icy lord of Kamakura inspired fear and respect but not affection.

Was Yoritomo suffering a fit of jealousy? Was he simply an older brother who felt that his annoyingly over-confident younger sibling needed a slap-down?

There is a darker possibility. By withholding honors from Yoshitsune, Yoritomo may have been digging a pit, lining it with sharp stakes, and counting on his proud and headstrong half brother to fall in.

In this rift between the two leading Minamoto, Go-Shirakawa spied an opportunity. By all accounts the Retired Emperor genuinely liked Yoshitsune. But he also wanted to blunt Yoritomo's growing power, and perhaps driving a wedge between Yoritomo and Yoshitsune would help. Six weeks after Yoshitsune's public humiliation, Go-Shirakawa offered him a title: Junior Lieutenant of the Outer Palace Guards.

Commanding the palace guards was a special honor and a mark of high favor. It offered a cooling salve for Yoshitsune's wounded pride. He accepted—without consulting Yoritomo.

When Yoritomo found out, he was furious. He had told his samurai not to accept any titles without his approval. Yoshitsune wrote to say that he had accepted only because he couldn't possibly refuse the Retired Emperor. They both knew it was a poor excuse.

In retaliation the lord of Kamakura took away Yoshitsune's military command and ordered Noriyori to lead the upcoming campaign against the Taira. Yoshitsune would stay in the capital, where he would find parties and poetry but no glory.

About six weeks later a small procession from Kamakura arrived at Yoshitsune's house in Kyoto. Maybe Yoritomo meant it as a peace offering; more likely it was another reminder of his dominance. The procession delivered to Yoshitsune the daughter of one of Yoritomo's retainers. Without debate or discussion Yoshitsune became a married man.

Far away on Yashima, the Taira guarded young Emperor Antoku and the imperial regalia. Yashima, an island crowned by a flat-topped mountain, was separated from the much larger island of Shikoku by shallow water. The Taira also had another base farther west, on the narrow straits of Dan-no-Ura. The straits separated the main Japanese island of Honshu from another island, Kyushu.

Noriyori decided to lead his troops toward Dan-no-Ura. Perhaps he calculated that Dan-no-Ura, although farther from Kyoto, offered easier access to the Taira. At Dan-no-Ura the straits separating Honshu and Kyushu were only a half mile wide. The crossing from Honshu to Yashima required three days of sailing.

While maple leaves reddened and fell, Noriyori's forces moved west. Their progress faltered as supplies from Kyoto took longer and longer to reach them. To compensate, the army behaved like heavily armed thugs, stealing rice and fodder from peasants along the way. Even their thievery wasn't enough to support thousands of men and horses.

Noriyori's warriors grew increasingly hungry and miserable. Sweat and rain seeped into the leather and lacing of their armor, turning it into a portable prison of lice and foul smells. By late fall Noriyori reported to Yoritomo that "because of the shortage of military provisions, the troops are listless, and more than half of them would welcome the opportunity to desert for their native provinces."

The lord of Kamakura had set aside his sharpest sword. However, by the beginning of 1185, Yoritomo could no longer tolerate Noriyori's incompetence. He unsheathed Yoshitsune.

After months of despair and inaction, Yoshitsune could barely contain himself. A quick and decisive victory at Yashima would surely erase Yoritomo's anger and allow reconciliation. Many happy rewards would follow.

Yoshitsune visited Go-Shirakawa to assure the Retired Emperor of his commitment to defeating the Taira—as if anyone could doubt it after his reckless ride down the cliffs at Ichi-no-Tani. Yoshitsune's ego was as big as ever. "I shall not return to the capital without destroying them, even if it means going as far as . . . Korea, India, or China," he promised. To his warriors Yoshitsune boasted, "I intend to attack by land as far as a horse can set foot, and by sea as far as an oar can reach."

At the beginning of the second month, Yoshitsune led three thousand Minamoto warriors out of Kyoto. Just two weeks later they arrived at a harbor on the Inland Sea. Local allies provided two hundred boats for the crossing to Shikoku. Unfortunately, it was a murderous time of year for sailing, and a strong, bone-chilling wind blew in from Siberia. The furious gale felled trees, whipped the waves into froth, and battered some of the Minamoto vessels.

While waiting for the damaged ships to be repaired,

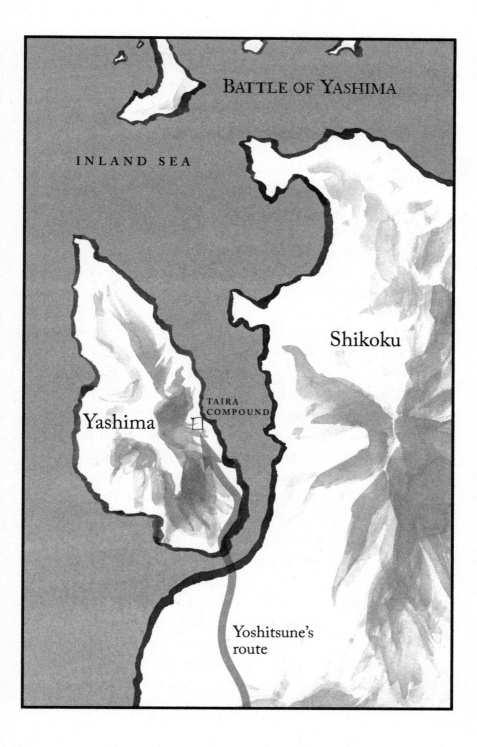

Yoshitsune argued with Yoritomo's closest retainer, Kage-toki. The lord of Kamakura had sent Kagetoki along to make sure Yoshitsune behaved. Kagetoki felt that his position as Yoritomo's right-hand man meant that Yoshitsune should defer to him. Yoshitsune, not surprisingly, saw things differently.

As usual, Yoshitsune asked his warriors' advice about the upcoming attack. Kagetoki suggested installing reverse oars on their vessels.

"What are reverse oars?" asked Yoshitsune, who knew very little about seamanship.

Kagetoki explained that while a rider could easily turn his horse around, a boatman couldn't turn a ship quickly. Installing extra oars and rudders mounted in a reverse fashion would allow the Minamoto to move backward even if there was no wind for the sails.

Yoshitsune retorted that he didn't plan to retreat. Kagetoki could put all the oars he wanted on *his* boat, but Yoshitsune would use "the usual equipment."

Kagetoki snapped back, "A good Commander-in-Chief gallops forward when he ought to and draws back when he ought to. . . . A rigid man is called a 'wild boar warrior'; people do not think much of him."

"I don't know anything about boars. . . . In battle, what I like is to attack flat out and win," said Yoshitsune.

Putting reverse oars on the boats was not a bad idea. However, most of the warriors disliked Kagetoki and adored Yoshitsune. No one dared laugh at Kagetoki, but the samurai threw amused glances at one another. Kagetoki noticed and did not forget.

Perhaps Yoshitsune, unable to confront Yoritomo himself, was taking out his frustrations on his half brother's favorite vassal. But he picked the worst of all possible enemies. The reverse-oars incident gave Kagetoki his first reason to hate Yoshitsune.

By nightfall the damaged Minamoto boats were repaired. Once again a gale-force wind blew up. Yoshitsune ordered his men to stock the vessels with provisions and weapons and load the warhorses. He wanted to leave immediately. Yoshitsune didn't bother to inform Kagetoki.

The boatmen protested. The fierce wind would be at their backs, yes, and would blow them straight across, but the waves were enormous. Conditions might be even worse farther out to sea. But Yoshitsune refused to listen. Claiming that the wind was simply "a little fresh," he gave his companions Tsuginobu and Ise Saburō an order. They stepped forward with drawn bows.

"Shoot down every one of those men if they don't launch the boats," Yoshitsune said.

The crews of five boats agreed to set sail. Satisfied, Yoshitsune didn't carry out his threat to kill the rest. It is said, "Whether out of fear of the wind or fear of Kagetoki, all the other vessels stayed behind." In any case, it may be that Yoshitsune preferred commanding a smaller force. "We must not tarry because others hold back," he told his companions.

One hundred fifty samurai and their horses boarded the five boats. Surely many were terrified to trust their lives to those stormy, shifting, dead-black waters. Yet they did. After all, some of them had already followed Yoshitsune off a cliff. And that had turned out well, hadn't it?

Yoshitsune didn't plan to sail directly to Yashima because he knew that the Taira, as experienced sailors, would have the advantage in any naval battle. He intended to land on Shikoku, cross the river separating Shikoku from Yashima, and surprise the Taira with a land assault.

Of course, for Yoshitsune's plan to work, the Minamoto had to survive the crossing.

Most Japanese vessels were nothing more than giant hollowed-out logs with boards attached to the sides, perhaps with a platform added to accommodate horses and other large cargo. The crafts were powered by oars and a single sail woven from reed or bamboo. Only a madman would take such fragile ships into a violent storm.

The Minamoto boats raced toward Shikoku with a wild wind at their backs. Oiled torches at the prow and stern of Yoshitsune's boat illuminated the appallingly large swells that lifted and dropped the vessels. Many of the Minamoto warriors probably spent the trip puking over the side or huddled between the horses. But eventually the sky lightened and the seas calmed. Yoshitsune and his men glimpsed the rounded islets that dot the water like lumps in batter, and by sunrise the mountainous bulk of Shikoku lined the horizon. With the storm wind at their backs, the samurai had made the three-day crossing in just six hours.

As the Minamoto drew closer to shore, they spotted red Taira banners. One hundred horsemen waited on the beach.

Yoshitsune knew his samurai would be vulnerable to Taira arrows when they anchored in the shallows to unload their warhorses. He ordered his men to force the saddled horses into the sea. The Minamoto kept their mounts swimming alongside the boats, held by lead lines, until the horses found footing. Yoshitsune and his men, screaming war cries, leaped over the sides of their ships and into their saddles. They charged out of the waves, lowering their heads and pulling their shoulder guards forward to deflect enemy arrows.

Instead of shooting, however, their opponents hastily retreated up the beach. Yoshitsune ordered his fearless friend Ise Saburō to bring back the group's leader. The leader, who turned out to be a local warrior unwilling to die for his Taira overlords, was willing to talk. The man told Yoshitsune that the beach where the Minamoto had landed was called Katsu-Ura: "Victory Beach."

Yoshitsune laughed and accused the samurai of trying to flatter him. The man insisted it was true.

"How far is it to Yashima from here?" Yoshitsune asked.

"Two days."

Yoshitsune decided to reach Yashima the next morning.

Using the local warrior as their guide, the Minamoto rode all day and all night, picking their way across a mountain range in utter darkness. By the following morning the band reached the waist-deep water separating Shikoku and Yashima. Yoshitsune ordered his men to set fire to nearby commoners' homes. Smoke roiled into the sky.

The Taira had anchored their fleet in a deep inlet off Yashima and built a walled compound on flat land nearby. The rising smoke sent the Taira leaders into a panic. A large Minamoto force had landed! There was no time to lose! Most retreated to their ships, taking along six-year-old Emperor Antoku and the imperial regalia.

The Taira watched anxiously as white Minamoto banners appeared through the morning haze. A group of five, another group of ten—Yoshitsune had ordered his samurai to arrive in small batches so the Taira would assume that a huge force was gradually filtering onto the beach.

Yoshitsune rode Tayūguro, the black stallion given to him by the Retired Emperor. His companions clustered around him: the warrior-monk Benkei, the brothers Tsuginobu and Tadanobu, and the former bandit Ise Saburō. The Taira aboard the boats sent arrows whizzing across the water at Yoshitsune and his horsemen. The Minamoto responded, shouting battle cries as they charged along the shoreline, firing at the men on the Taira ships. Tsuginobu and Tadanobu burst into the Taira compound and set it on fire.

Too late, the Taira realized that the Minamoto force was actually quite small. Kiyomori's son Munemori, the leader of the Taira, ordered some of his warriors into small boats. They rowed close to the burned-out main gate of the compound. Yoshitsune and his men retreated out of arrow range.

A Taira shouted from the prow of his boat: "Who is the Honorable Commander-in-Chief of the [Minamoto] today?"

Ise Saburō walked his horse forward. He said it was Yoshitsune, younger brother of the lord of Kamakura.

The Taira warrior sneered. He called Yoshitsune a stripling orphan, a former temple servant who had tramped off to Hiraizumi "as a gold merchant's lackey, carrying provisions on his back."

Trash talk, it seems, is not a modern invention.

"Keep your big mouth shut about my master!" Ise Saburō snapped. He said the Taira survived by begging and sniveling.

"They tell me you support yourself and your family by [banditry]," the Taira shouted.

As insults flew back and forth, one of Yoshitsune's men shot an arrow into the Taira's chest. "So ended the battle of words," the war chronicle notes drily.

Kiyomori's nephew Noritsune had listened to the exchange with growing fury. He had ample reason for thoughts of revenge: two of his brothers had died at Ichi-no-Tani. Like Yoshitsune, Noritsune was twenty-six years old. Unlike Yoshitsune, Noritsune was famous for his archery skills.

When his fellow Taira fell dead beside him, Noritsune realized that their enemies were not *quite* out of range. It was easy enough to identify Yoshitsune. The Minamoto commander-in-chief was surely the one who wore purple-laced armor, carried a sword with gilt fittings, and sat atop a flashy gold-edged saddle.

Noritsune swept an arrow from his quiver, took aim, and let his hatred fly.

9

THE DROPPED BOW

Noritsune's drawn bow caught the attention of Tsuginobu, Tadanobu, Benkei, and Ise Saburō. They jerked their horses' heads around in a desperate attempt to get between the arrow and Yoshitsune. Noritsune's shot hit Tsuginobu's left shoulder and drove all the way through his body. Yoshitsune's friend toppled off his mount and collapsed in the sand.

Noritsune continued to fire a furious barrage of arrows. The Minamoto whirled their horses, pushing Yoshitsune out of range. Noritsune's teenage servant jumped from his boat and sprinted through the shallows toward the dying Tsuginobu. The boy carried a naginata and clearly intended to slash off Tsuginobu's head and bring it back to Noritsune. Tsuginobu's older brother, Tadanobu, spun his horse and drew. His arrow struck a joint of the boy's armor and plunged deep into his body. The teenager dropped to his hands and knees.

Noritsune leaped from his boat and dragged the

mortally wounded boy away. Minamoto samurai dismounted and carried Tsuginobu out of range.

They laid the dying man on the beach. Yoshitsune held Tsuginobu's hand as his friend took his last breath. It could not have been the first time Yoshitsune watched a good man die. Yet it may have been the first death to stab his heart.

Word of Yoshitsune's arrival had spread quickly across Shikoku. All morning, groups of local samurai who wanted to join the Minamoto filtered onto the beach, adding their numbers to Yoshitsune's small force. Yet the standoff remained. The Taira didn't want to give up Yashima, but they were reluctant to take on Yoshitsune's skilled horsemen. As the Taira ships bobbed at anchor, agonizingly out of reach, Yoshitsune could only watch in frustration.

Morning lapsed into afternoon. At last the Taira rowed a small vessel within a few hundred feet of shore and turned it broadside. A young woman in bright-red and green robes emerged from a small cabin and planted a pole on deck. Fixed to the top of the pole was a red fan. She beckoned the Minamoto, as if to ask, *Is there an archer among you who can hit this target?*

Was it a taunt? Or a trick? Maybe the Taira wanted to lure Yoshitsune into arrow range again. Whatever the Taira intention, Yoshitsune decided that Minamoto pride was at stake. The challenge must be answered.

The Minamoto's best archer was a young man just twenty years old. It is said that when shooting birds in flight—the most difficult of targets—he could hit two out of every three. Yoshitsune ordered the young man to shoot the fan. When the youth tried to decline, Yoshitsune flew into a rage.

"You men who have left Kamakura for the west must obey my orders," he snapped. "If anyone wants to haggle, let him go home right now."

Perhaps it's not surprising that Yoshitsune's mood had turned ugly. He hadn't slept more than a few hours in the past three days. His enemies remained beyond his reach. And one of his closest friends lay dead, killed by an arrow meant for him.

The young archer dared not refuse a second time. He rode his horse into the water. A strong wind blew and waves slapped his horse's chest. The fan atop the pole twitched unsteadily in the breeze; the boat lurched up and down with the swells. The Taira crowded the sides of their boats to watch while the Minamoto lined their mounts bridle to bridle on the beach.

Samurai archers used many different kinds of arrowheads: forked shapes for cutting ropes, half-moon shapes for cutting throats, and turnip-shaped bulbs that whistled or hummed to distract enemy troops or signal allies. Since this was theater, not battle, the Minamoto youth chose a humming bulb. He murmured a prayer and closed his eyes. When he opened them again, the wind seemed to have faded. He took the shot.

The arrow sang as it flew. It struck the fan near the base, severing it from the pole. For a moment the fan fluttered in the breeze. Then it dropped into the sea, floating in the waves like an oversized autumn leaf.

The Taira beat the sides of their boats in applause; the Minamoto shouted and slapped their quivers. A warrior emerged from the cabin of the boat and began to dance on the deck with a naginata.

Ise Saburō rode his horse over to the young Minamoto archer and told him that Yoshitsune wanted the dancer shot. The performance ended abruptly when the Minamoto's arrow pierced the dancer's neck. He thudded into the bottom of the boat.

Some of the Minamoto roared in approval; others were shocked. But the dancer's death worked as Yoshitsune probably intended. Several hundred furious Taira landed their boats on the beach and gathered behind standing shields the size of small doors, "overlapped like a hen's folded wings."

Finally, enemies within striking distance! With his companions gathered around him, flanked by Tadanobu and Ise Saburō, Yoshitsune shouted a war cry and galloped his black stallion straight at the Taira.

The Minamoto charge shattered the Taira line. Minamoto warhorses kicked, trampled, and scattered shields. Those Taira who survived the first assault broke ranks and fled to their rowboats as Yoshitsune and his men rode their horses belly-deep into the sea in pursuit, firing arrows all the while. The shallows churned with flailing oars, bellowing men, and whirling horses. Heedless of the danger, Yoshitsune drove the attack closer and closer to the Taira boats.

Those aboard spied an opportunity. Taira samurai grabbed iron-clawed kumade and swung them at Yoshitsune. His companions tried to knock them aside with their swords. Amid the chaos a claw snagged Yoshitsune's bow and ripped it from his hand. It splashed into the water.

Instead of backing away, Yoshitsune leaned out of his saddle and tried to fish his bow out of the water with his riding whip. His men shouted, "Let it go!"

Yoshitsune ignored them. At last, having snared his bow, he wheeled Tayūguro around and rode back to shore, laughing like a maniac.

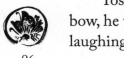

His men followed. Some of his friends berated him for such recklessness. What was his bow worth, compared to his life?

"I would have been glad to relinquish it if it had been one like my Uncle Tametomo's, which needed two or three men for the stringing: I might even have dropped it on purpose," Yoshitsune replied. "I risked my life for it because I was unwilling to let an enemy recover a weak weapon and sneer, 'This bow belonged to . . . Yoshitsune.'"

It did make a crazy kind of sense.

By then the winter sun was sinking. With no way to end the standoff, Yoshitsune and his warriors moved off the beach, splashed back across the shallows, and made camp on Shikoku. Every man was exhausted. Still, Yoshitsune knew the Taira might try to overwhelm them during the night. It was exactly the sort of thing *he* would do. Most of the weary warriors pillowed their heads on their helmets, armor sleeves, or quivers and fell into exhausted sleep. But at least two men remained on watch. Ise Saburō hid in a ditch with his bow and a supply of arrows. If their enemies attacked, he planned to shoot their warhorses in the belly. Yoshitsune settled atop a nearby hill.

The Taira leadership discussed their options. Still seething at his failure to kill Yoshitsune, the archer Noritsune asked to lead five hundred samurai in a midnight attack against Yoshitsune's forces. But the Taira debated and dithered, unable to agree who should command. The night passed.

The next morning the Taira fleet sailed into a bay on Shikoku, where the Minamoto spotted them. Yoshitsune handpicked a strike force of eighty men and rode to the shoreline, guessing that at least some of the Taira warriors would leave their ships if he offered himself as bait. He knew they wanted his head very, very badly.

Certain that they could crush eighty horsemen, hundreds of Taira piled into rowboats and landed on the shore. On cue the rest of Yoshitsune's horsemen poured out of the surrounding hills. The stunned Taira assumed that the full Minamoto army had just arrived to reinforce Yoshitsune. After a brief skirmish they once again retreated to their ships. Once again Yoshitsune could not follow. The Taira leadership, along with little Emperor Antoku and the Japanese regalia, sailed out of his reach.

Yoshitsune could still comfort himself with a remarkable success. He had flushed the Taira off Yashima and denied them Shikoku as well. Every Taira loss, every Taira retreat, encouraged more western lords to switch their allegiance to the Minamoto.

Yet one task remained.

Yoshitsune and his companions buried their friend Tsuginobu in a field of pine stumps. The warrior from Hiraizumi had left his northern home, crossed the Uji River, ridden over a cliff, sailed through a tempest, and taken an arrow—all for Yoshitsune. As a Buddhist, Yoshitsune believed that someday his friend's soul would be reincarnated. The merit Tsuginobu had earned in this life through his loyalty and faithfulness would ensure his high birth and happiness in the next.

Yoshitsune asked his men to summon a monk from a nearby temple. He gave the holy man his stallion Tayūguro and his gold-edged saddle; in exchange the monk promised to copy and recite Buddhist scriptures to soothe Tsuginobu's soul. Yoshitsune's horse and saddle were probably the most valuable things he owned—maybe the *only* valuable things he owned. The gesture brought tears to the eyes of his warriors.

A few days later Kagetoki finally made it across the Inland Sea with the rest of the Minamoto army. Yoshitsune's companions smugly pointed out that Yoshitsune had already conquered Yashima and Shikoku. They joked that they didn't need Kagetoki, who was now "as useless as altar-flowers picked too late for the rite."

Kagetoki tallied his second reason to hate Yoshitsune.

The Taira now had one sanctuary left: their base at Dan-no-Ura, the narrow waterway separating the islands of Honshu and Kyushu. A sea battle at Dan-no-Ura could end the war once and for all.

Messengers streamed from Kamakura as Yoritomo ordered his allies in the west to supply provisions, men, and ships for the final assault. Anyone who wanted their land rights confirmed must heed Yoritomo's call. It escaped no one's notice that Yoritomo had the power to confiscate Taira estates and dole them out to those who supported him.

The lord of Kamakura put Yoshitsune in charge of the assault on Dan-no-Ura. Yoshitsune's victories usually depended on surprise attacks executed with small bands of horsemen. The battle of Dan-no-Ura would be fought at sea with hundreds of boats and thousands of men. There would be no horses. No element of surprise. No familiar ground—in fact, no ground at all.

Taira confidence grew. "The eastern warriors may talk big on horseback, but when did they learn to fight on water?" scoffed a Taira lord. "They will be like fish that have tried to climb trees."

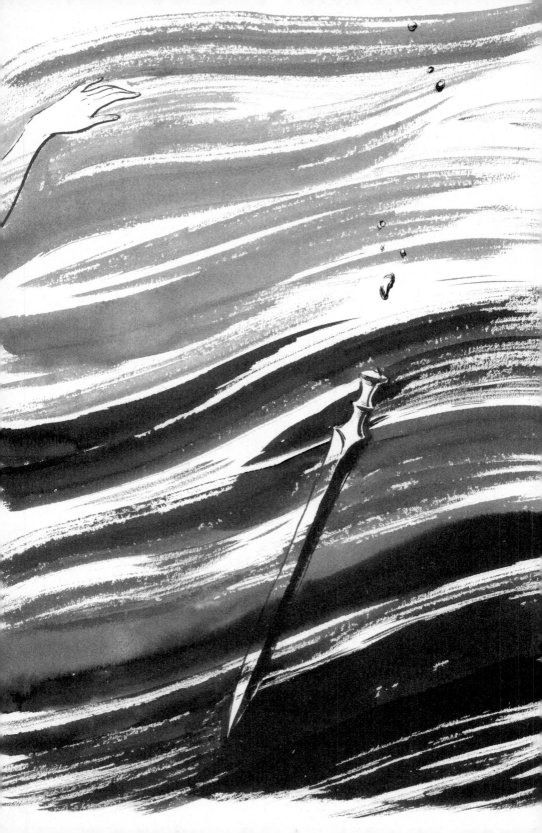

IO

THE DROWNED SWORD

DAN-NO-URA, 1185

It took Yoshitsune about a month to organize his ragtag fleet. We don't know his exact route, but he probably moved steadily west from port to port along the southern coast of Honshu. Along the way he joined his forces with his half brother Noriyori's and amassed eight hundred boats and thousands of samurai—most of them former Taira allies who had just switched their allegiance to the Minamoto. It was a navy of the disloyal.

Yoshitsune's vessels weren't warships. Most were probably oared sailing boats forty or fifty feet long, sometimes with a small cabin on the stern deck. The Minamoto prepared for battle by lashing planks to the sides of their ships to shield their archers. They stocked the vessels with arrows, naginata, kumade, rakes, and grappling hooks.

The Taira, led by Kiyomori's son Munemori, commanded about five hundred vessels. Most of their ships resembled the Minamoto's. However, the Taira fleet also included several Chinese-style ships. These larger, taller vessels could ram and crush smaller boats. And the towering multilevel structures on their decks provided perfect archers' platforms. The Minamoto suspected that one of the Chinese-style vessels contained the most critical cargo: little Emperor Antoku and the imperial regalia.

The Minamoto fleet carried about three to four thousand fighting men. The Taira fleet contained between four and five thousand.

Heavy spring rain delayed the arrival of the Minamoto fleet at Dan-no-Ura. But at last the weather cleared. Early on the final morning, as the Taira waited just a few miles away, Yoshitsune gathered his commanders for a final strategy session. Yoritomo's right-hand man, Kagetoki, joined in.

Kagetoki liked to tell a story about one of his ancestors. When Kagetoki's forefather was shot in the eye by a barbarian king, he had pulled the arrow out and shot it back, killing the barbarian instantly. Perhaps with this macho heritage in mind, Kagetoki asked Yoshitsune to let him lead the assault on the Taira.

"I might if I were not going to be there myself," Yoshitsune responded.

Kagetoki reminded him that as commander-in-chief, Yoshitsune shouldn't risk his life by fighting on the front line. Yoshitsune retorted that his half brother Yoritomo was actually the commander-in-chief, so he and Kagetoki were equally expendable. This wasn't true, of course. But when pride arrives, logic takes a hike.

Kagetoki muttered, "This lord lacks what it takes to be a leader of men!"

Yoshitsune overheard. He put his hand on his sword hilt and snapped, "You are the biggest fool in Japan!"

Kagetoki's three sons surrounded their father. Benkei, Tadanobu, and Ise Saburō moved forward to protect Yoshitsune. Other samurai lords grabbed Kagetoki and Yoshitsune and pleaded with them: a fight within the Minamoto leadership would only help their enemies. And what would the lord of Kamakura think?

Both Kagetoki and Yoshitsune calmed down. But Kagetoki checked off a third reason to hate Yoshitsune.

The straits of Dan-no-Ura rest between mountainous is-lands: Kyushu on one side and Honshu on the other. The Minamoto fleet approached from the east, moving toward the narrowest part of the straits, where the sea was no more than a half mile wide. The Taira fleet waited for them there. They knew that the strong tide flowing through the straits that morning would give them an advantage. It would carry them toward the Minamoto and increase their vessels' speed. The Minamoto would be fighting not only the Taira but also the backward drag of the tide.

Sea winds whipped the banners festooning the ships: red for the Taira and white for the Minamoto. The vessel commanded by Kagetoki sailed close to shore, where the tidal flow was weakest, and slipped ahead of the rest of the Minamoto fleet. His men snagged a passing Taira vessel with rakes. Kagetoki, his sons, and several retainers jumped aboard. The party ranged from bow to stern with drawn swords, cutting down everyone in their path. And

BATTLE OF DAN-NO-URA

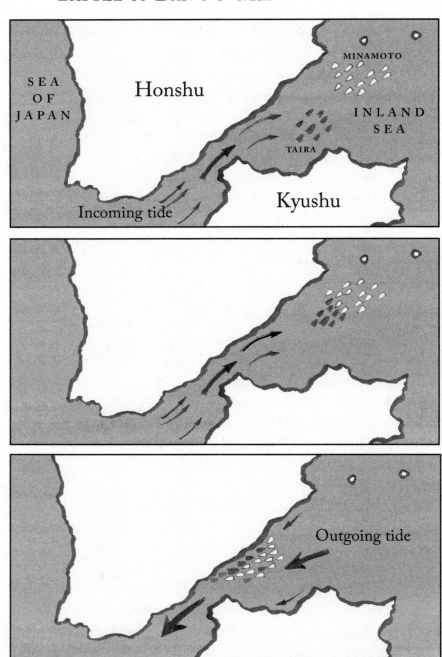

so Kagetoki did manage to seize the honor of being the first to attack.

The Taira commanders weren't concerned by Kagetoki's small victory. They wanted Yoshitsune. Taira samurai were ordered to target any high-ranking Minamoto who was "fair-skinned and short with buck teeth." One Taira warrior conceded that Yoshitsune was "a fighter," but added, "He's too small to bother anyone. I'll just clap him under my arm and throw him in."

The best Taira archers lined the bows of the ships. As soon as they drew within range of the lead Minamoto vessels—Yoshitsune naturally insisted on sailing in the vanguard—they released a barrage of arrows. Shafts studded shields and armor; dead and wounded Minamoto thudded to the decks.

The Taira beat their attack drums and raised a victory shout. "Our side is winning!"

As the Taira assault punctured the Minamoto front line, other Taira vessels fanned out to encircle Yoshitsune's ships. Boats crashed together. Warriors used grappling hooks to lash their ships to enemy vessels, turning the battleground into a heaving, shifting checkerboard of blood-slickened decks. Samurai swarmed across one another's boats, fighting hand to hand with swords, naginata, and daggers. Sometimes a warrior simply shoved his heavily armored opponent into the sea. All the while the tide carried the Minamoto toward the rocky shore of Honshu. The Minamoto rowed hard and battled harder but could not overcome their fatal backward drift. For the first time in his life, Yoshitsune fought on the defensive.

Doubt spread through the Minamoto ranks. What if the gods sided with those who carried Emperor Antoku and the imperial regalia?

A Minamoto banner tore loose. Swept up by the wind, the white cloth drifted like a cloud past Yoshitsune's ship. Yoshitsune told his men to take heart: Hachiman, patron god of the Minamoto, had sent them a promise of victory. But the Taira continued to press hard. They knew they had to crush the Minamoto before the tide switched direction.

In the middle of this desperate struggle, the Minamoto captured the son of a high-ranking Taira ally. The boy's father swiftly surrendered. He offered vital information in exchange for his son's life. He explained that neither the Taira commanders, nor Emperor Antoku, nor the imperial regalia were aboard those impressive Chinese-style ships. The big ships were bait. When the Minamoto attacked the Chinese-style ships, the Taira leaders—who secretly commanded the fighting from small boats nearby—intended to surround and annihilate their enemies. The man offered to point out the Taira command boats as well as the vessel carrying the child emperor and the imperial regalia.

Something else happened in that hour. Heeding the tug of the unseen moon, not the tiny struggles of men, the tide slowed. It stopped. It turned.

Without the tide's help the Taira couldn't push Yoshitsune's ships into the rocks. Now the Minamoto ships could maneuver and pick up speed. One by one they broke free of the Taira encirclement. Yoshitsune ordered his archers to pick off the rowers and helmsmen on the boats carrying the Taira leaders. Bodies piled on the decks as the targeted vessels veered helplessly out of control.

As the tide and the momentum of the battle shifted, so did allegiances. Many samurai treated the notion of loyalty as a suggestion rather than an iron principle. Some of the Taira allies shamelessly switched to the Minamoto side right in the middle of the battle. "Yesterday's subordinates wielded bows against their sovereign," says the war chronicle, "and drew swords against their masters."

One of Taira Kiyomori's sons realized the end was near. He rowed to the ship carrying Emperor Antoku. When the women aboard anxiously asked how the battle was going, he laughed and said sarcastically, "You will be getting acquainted with some remarkable eastern warriors."

Kiyomori's widow didn't wait for the Minamoto to arrive. She took the sacred imperial sword and stuck it into her sash. It was a sword of the ancient style, straight and double-edged. According to legend, the brother of the sun goddess had cut off a sea dragon's tail and discovered the sword inside. He gave the sacred sword to his sister, who gave it to her descendants, who became the first emperors of Japan. With the mythic sword at her side, Kiyomori's widow gathered her grandson into her arms and walked to the side of the ship.

"Where are you taking me, Grandmother?" asked little Antoku.

"This land of ours, a few millet grains scattered in remote seas, is not a nice place. I am taking you to a happier one, the Pure Land of Bliss," Kiyomori's widow said, weeping. "Down there, far beneath the waves, another capital awaits us."

Still holding her grandson, she stepped over the side and plunged into the sea.

Emperor Antoku's mother jumped in after them, her robes flowering around her as she sank. She did not sink quickly enough. A Minamoto warrior snagged the long stream of her hair with a kumade claw and dragged her into his boat.

Minamoto scrambled aboard the imperial vessel. A lady grabbed the chest containing the sacred mirror and tried to throw herself into the sea, but a quick-thinking samurai shot an arrow that pinned her skirt to the side of the ship. She tripped and fell, and the chest was snatched away. Another Taira threw the box holding the sacred jewel into the water but neglected to weight it down. The precious package bobbed in the waves until a Minamoto fished it out.

Despair swept through the Taira ranks. Some of the commanders feared the dishonor of capture so much that they chose to drown instead. Two of Kiyomori's brothers weighted themselves with small anchors and dived into the sea; three of Kiyomori's grandsons followed with linked hands. Yet the Taira commander-in-chief, Kiyomori's son Munemori, showed no such resolve. He lingered on his ship with his teenage son. Munemori's men were so embarrassed that they gave their leader a helpful shove. After his father splashed into the sea, Munemori's son jumped in.

Both Munemori and his son were strong swimmers and didn't sink despite their heavy armor. They were still bobbing in the swells when Yoshitsune's friend Ise Saburō, accompanied by several other samurai, rowed over in a small boat. They dragged the Taira from the water.

A foster brother of Munemori's spotted the capture. He pulled alongside, jumped into the boat, and killed one of Ise Saburō's men. As he raged toward Ise Saburō, another Minamoto shot him in the face with an arrow.

Other Taira also refused to quit—including Kiyomori's nephew, the famous archer Noritsune. The Taira cause might be lost, but he could still seek revenge. He had failed to kill Yoshitsune at Yashima. He did not intend to fail again.

By then Noritsune had exhausted his supply of arrows. So with a naginata in one hand and a sword in the other, he ranged from boat to boat, "suspecting anyone finely equipped," hunting for Yoshitsune's head.

At last Noritsune spied his prey. Yoshitsune stood on a Minamoto ship holding a naginata. No one guarded the Minamoto commander-in-chief. Ise Saburō was rowing around plucking prize Taira from the water; Benkei and Tadanobu were also away from Yoshitsune's side. Perhaps, like Ise Saburō, they had yielded to the temptation to go fishing for high-ranking heads. Whatever the reason, Yoshitsune was unprotected.

Yoshitsune saw the Taira vessel approach and spotted Noritsune aboard. He strode across the deck of his own boat toward his enemy. The two ships drew near . . .

With a shout of triumph, Noritsune leaped into Yoshitsune's boat.

ASSASSINS IN THE DARK

Dan-no-Ura, Kyoto, and Koshigoe, 1185

In a normal story one of two things would happen. Version one: The two enemies engage in a long, drawn-out fight. Desperate and backed against the side of his ship, our hard-pressed hero is seemingly overmatched by his bigger, stronger enemy. With some amazingly clever trick, however, Yoshitsune kills Noritsune and wins the day.

Version two: The two enemies engage in a long, drawn-out fight. Despite a valiant battle, Noritsune kills our hero. Although tragic, this ending also satisfies. The cosmic scales, so heavily weighted toward the Minamoto, now tilt back toward the vanquished Taira in a sad but satisfying way.

The truth is different, and more revealing.

Yoshitsune's move in Noritsune's direction was simply a feint. As soon as Noritsune jumped onto the deck of Yoshitsune's ship, Yoshitsune coolly tucked his naginata under his arm and nimbly leaped into a passing Minamoto vessel. Apparently the two ships were moving apart, because when Noritsune rushed to follow, the watery gap was already too wide to jump.

Noritsune went berserk. He threw his naginata and his sword into the sea and tore off his helmet and the skirts of his armor. When three Minamoto samurai approached him, Noritsune kicked one overboard and grabbed the other two, one under each arm.

"Fine, you're coming with me," he cried, and toppled over the side with his victims. The cold, choppy waters closed over their heads.

After Noritsune's suicide the fighting slowed. The last of the Taira leaders joined Noritsune in the depths. Some tied on two sets of armor just to make sure they wouldn't be captured like spineless Munemori. When all fighting stopped, the survivors gazed at the carnage. The red banners and badges of the Taira, it is said, floated on the sea like leaves scattered by an autumn storm. Boats drifted with their burden of bodies. And in the dark waters below, bottom-feeders dined on the dead.

Yoritomo was still negotiating with several important western lords when news of the stunning victory arrived from Yoshitsune. Without question Minamoto Yoritomo was now the most powerful samurai in Japan.

Yoshitsune also sent word to Go-Shirakawa. The Retired Emperor immediately fired off his congratulations to Yoshitsune but waited a few days before dispatching a similar message to Yoritomo. This did not go unnoticed by the lord of Kamakura.

Messengers returned to Noriyori and Yoshitsune with orders from Yoritomo. Noriyori would remain in the west to administer lands confiscated from the Taira and was instructed to "make every effort to retrieve the Sacred Sword."

Noriyori sent women divers down to search the gray waters, but the sea refused to give up its treasure. People remembered how the sword had been cut from the tail of a sea dragon. Surely, they whispered, Emperor Antoku was the sea dragon reincarnated, and the little boy's drowning was just a way of bringing the sword home.

Back in Kyoto another emperor had already been named. Go-Toba was a four-year-old grandson of Go-Shirakawa's. The imperial court had broken with tradition and enthroned the boy without waiting for the return of the imperial regalia.

The lord of Kamakura sent new orders to Yoshitsune. He was instructed to return to Kyoto with Munemori, Munemori's son, and other high-ranking Taira prisoners.

Yoshitsune's party moved east at the plodding pace of oxcarts loaded with captives. There seemed to be no real hurry now that the fighting was over. During the month-long journey, Yoshitsune probably basked in well-earned praise and dreamed of a secure and happy future. Surely his great victory would erase all bad feelings between him and his half brother. Old mistakes would be forgiven and forgotten. *Now* Yoritomo would recognize and reward him.

Yet Yoshitsune had made enemies. What looked like daring to Yoshitsune's admirers was described as reckless-ness by his detractors. It did not help that by this time Yoshitsune probably had an ego the size of Mount Fuji.

Many high-ranking Minamoto felt overshadowed by Yoshitsune—including, of course, Kagetoki. Yoritomo once praised his favorite vassal as "most adept with words,"

113

and Kagetoki used this skill against Yoshitsune. As Yoshitsune rode at a leisurely pace to Kyoto, Kagetoki secretly sent one of his relatives racing to Kamakura with a devastating letter. It read in part:

> *Although Yoshitsune is of the opinion that the victory was due to his efforts alone, I ask, was it not the result of the cooperative efforts of a large force? Every member of this large force has been motivated by a desire to serve, not Yoshitsune, but the ruler. This was the reason for the cooperative spirit and the great achievement. However, after the destruction of the [Taira], Yoshitsune's pride has only increased, so that the very existence of his followers is endangered. He does not tolerate contrary opinions and refuses to compromise. I, as one close to your Lordship, and as one who knows Yoshitsune's inclination toward arbitrariness, have cautioned him, each time that he has acted in this manner, that such conduct would not be pleasing to your Lordship. But, instead, these words of counsel have become cause for reprisal, and I may even be punished for them. Now that the war has been completed, I beg your leave to be recalled to Kamakura and to terminate my attendance on Yoshitsune.*

Yoshitsune arrived in Kyoto near the end of the fourth month of 1185. The Taira prisoners and their Minamoto guards would follow a few days later. As part of his victory lap, Yoshitsune proudly restored the sacred jewel and the sacred mirror to the imperial family. The court gave him the honor of holding a torch aloft as the mirror was paraded into the imperial palace. The mirror, of course, had to remain locked in the darkness of a chest. As everyone knew, it had once reflected the face of the sun goddess and now only the emperor could look into it without being blinded or paralyzed.

During the ceremony to welcome the sacred mirror, Yoshitsune wore the uniform of an imperial policeman under his armor—a reminder of the junior lieutenant rank given him by the Retired Emperor in defiance of Yoritomo. Unfortunately, word of Yoshitsune's clothing choice got back to Kamakura.

Kagetoki's venomous letter wasn't the only one to arrive. Noriyori wrote to Yoritomo to complain that Yoshitsune had tried to govern Kyushu after Dan-no-Ura, even though Kyushu was supposed to be Noriyori's responsibility. It was as if little demons kept visiting Yoritomo's shoulder to whisper, *Yoshitsune is arrogant and headstrong. He can't be trusted. He'll try to seize power.*

Back in Kyoto the high-ranking Taira captives rolled through the streets in wickerwork oxcarts. Thousands lined the streets to gawk. Aristocrats turned out, too, though they remained inside sleek black-lacquered carriages hung with blinds and brocade curtains for privacy. Even Retired Emperor Go-Shirakawa attended.

For years the Taira had inspired fear and resentment. Now many people pitied the captives. Kiyomori's son Munemori, once a handsome man, had become thin and worn. He was no doubt painfully aware of the disgrace he had brought upon the Taira by not dying at Dan-no-Ura. During the procession a former servant of Munemori's approached Yoshitsune to ask if he could guide his former master's oxcart one last time. Yoshitsune agreed. The man cried so hard, however, that he could barely hold the rope as the ox lumbered down the street.

The unhappy parade ended at Yoshitsune's residence on Rokujō (Sixth Avenue). The captives would remain under Yoshitsune's guardianship until the lord of Kamakura determined their fate. Twenty-five years earlier, Taira Kiyomori had faced the same decision about Yoritomo and Yoshitsune.

Around this time Yoshitsune got wind of the smear campaign against him. He tried sending a messenger to Yoritomo with assurances of his loyalty, but the letter did nothing to mend the rupture. Yoritomo found it suspicious that Yoshitsune had declared his loyalty only *after* learning of Yoritomo's displeasure with him. Of course, Yoshitsune had no reason to believe that a loyalty pledge was necessary. Hadn't he dedicated his entire life to restoring Minamoto glory? Hadn't he done everything asked of him with extraordinary speed and skill? Didn't he deserve credit for the military victories that had made the lord of Kamakura the most powerful samurai in Japan?

Yoshitsune was no doubt stunned to discover— shortly after writing his letter—that Yoritomo had already decided to remove him as commander-in-chief of the Minamoto army. According to Yoritomo, Yoshitsune "had abused his commission as [Yoritomo's] representative in the west and had caused resentment among [Yoritomo's] vassals who had been assigned to his command by demanding of them complete subservience to him."

There was nothing Yoshitsune could do. His elder half brother was the leader of the Minamoto. It was his army, not Yoshitsune's. Yoshitsune was the Minamoto's star quarterback, so to speak, but Yoritomo owned the team. And the stadium. Yoshitsune didn't even have a large network of personal retainers. All he had was his small misfit band that included Benkei, Ise Saburō, Tadanobu, and Washinoo, the teenage hunter who had joined his team at Ichi-no-Tani.

The victor of Uji River, Ichi-no-Tani, Yashima, and Dan-no-Ura now endured the same purgatory as the Taira prisoners who lived as his unwilling houseguests. Everyone waited for word from Kamakura.

Perhaps this explains Yoshitsune's marriage. Already wed to the daughter of one of Yoritomo's vassals, and already involved with Shizuka, the famous shirabyōshi dancer, twenty-six-year-old Yoshitsune took the daughter of one of the Taira captives as his second wife. We don't know her name, but she was said to be lovely and sweet-tempered—though at twenty-three considered "a little old."

Yoshitsune did not bother to seek the lord of Kamakura's blessing.

Life in Kyoto gradually returned to normal. The aristocrats celebrated the annual Iris Festival by watching horse races and wearing lush garlands of irises believed to ward off illness. Across the city the smell of raw wood filled the air as carpenters, roof tilers, and stonecutters rebuilt ruined homes. Peddlers of charcoal, firewood, and oil strolled down the avenues calling out their wares as puppeteers and monkey trainers entertained on street corners. Craftspeople went back to work weaving silk, lacquering hats, forging swords, and carving Buddhas. Merchants jingling copper Chinese coins returned to the long, shaded stalls of the marketplace. Kyoto's citizens had good reason to praise

Yoshitsune, the man who had so swiftly ended the ruinous civil war.

A message arrived ordering Yoshitsune to bring Munemori and his teenage son to Kamakura. This was Yoshitsune's big opportunity. A face-to-face reunion with Yoritomo—their first meeting in seventeen months— would allow Yoshitsune to clear his name. They were half brothers, after all, and together had accomplished great things. The lord of Kamakura might be the steel backbone of the Minamoto, but Yoshitsune was the cutting edge.

We can imagine Yoshitsune allowing himself these hopes as he rode east to Kamakura. But when his party arrived at Koshigoe, a government checkpoint just a few miles outside the city, Yoritomo's father-in-law was waiting. He told Yoshitsune that the Taira prisoners would receive an audience with the lord of Kamakura. Yoshitsune would not.

Yoshitsune may have told himself that this was the lord of Kamakura's way of disciplining him. Surely his half brother would relent after a day or two.

Eight days passed. Yoshitsune sent an anxious letter to a retainer of Yoritomo's—someone he thought might be sympathetic to his plight.

> *Minamoto Yoshitsune, Junior Lieutenant, Left Division, of the Outer Palace Guards, most humbly addresses you. . . . Whereas I have demonstrated the skill of generations of military training and have cleansed the family of its past disgrace and should, hence, be singled out for honors; instead, my prodigious deeds, because of unexpectedly vicious slander, have been ignored. While I have done no wrong, I have been reproached. I have committed no mistakes*

and am deserving; yet I have incurred your dis-
pleasure, and I weep crimson tears in vain. . . . At
such a time, if I do not gaze upon my brother's kind
face, there is no meaning in the bond of kindred
brotherhood. . . . Use your excellent discretion and
acquaint my brother with the fact that I have com-
mitted no wrong.

When the letter was read to Yoritomo, he made no comment. The official record says only: "Action is expected later."

Yoritomo kept Yoshitsune waiting for twenty-five days. At last, guards returned with Munemori, his teenage son, and an order from Yoritomo: Yoshitsune must execute the two prisoners on their way back to Kyoto. A meeting with the lord of Kamakura was denied.

The Taira captives lived a few more days only because their heads needed to be fresh so their faces would be recognizable. Yoshitsune's men decapitated Taira Munemori and his son a few miles outside the capital. The heads were carried into Kyoto and hung from the trees beside the prison gate.

The steady erosion of Yoshitsune's status continued. Yoritomo had earlier given Yoshitsune several parcels of land seized from the Taira, probably to provide him with enough rental income to pay his expenses in Kyoto. By the time Yoshitsune returned to his mansion on Rokujō, his farmland had been confiscated. Insult by insult, the lord of Kamakura seemed to be trying to goad his half brother into open rebellion.

Yoshitsune sweated and stewed through the swampy weather of late summer. Yet he still refused to make any threatening moves against Yoritomo. There are many possible explanations for this man of action's sudden inaction. Yoshitsune may have suffered from illness or depression. Perhaps his aristocratic friends, including Go-Shirakawa, counseled him to lie low; Yoritomo's anger would eventually cool. It is also possible that Yoshitsune couldn't bring himself to rebel because he truly believed in Minamoto honor and family loyalty. Unfortunately for Yoshitsune, his half brother was capable of six nasty things before breakfast.

On the ninth day of the seventh month, at eleven o'clock in the morning, the ground below Kyoto buckled and shook. Earthen walls crumbled, tall pagodas tipped, and roof ridges snapped and sagged. A cloud of dust thrown up by collapsing buildings boiled into the sky. Taira Kiyomori had become a dragon, people said, and was shaking the capital with his anger. If he existed as a spirit of vengeance, Kiyomori was a spectacularly incompetent one: Yoshitsune's Kyoto residence remained undamaged.

About six weeks after the earthquake, a messenger from the lord of Kamakura arrived on Yoshitsune's doorstep. It was Kagetoki's eldest son. There could be no more bitter reminder that Kagetoki—not Yoshitsune—had the ear of the lord of Kamakura.

At first Yoshitsune's servants refused Kagetoki's son entry. Their lord was ill, they said, too ill for visitors. It was several days before Yoshitsune agreed to see him.

Kagetoki's son already knew Yoshitsune. He had stood threateningly beside his father, ready to kill, during the bitter argument between Kagetoki and Yoshitsune over who should have the honor of first attack at

Dan-no-Ura. Now, when brought before Yoshitsune, Kagetoki's son was shocked. Yoshitsune's high energy had vanished. Thin and weak, he leaned heavily on an armrest. Kagetoki's son glimpsed burn scars on Yoshitsune. In those days a common medical treatment involved burning herbs on the patient's skin.

Kagetoki's son told Yoshitsune that the lord of Kamakura had a job for him. To prove his loyalty, Yoshitsune must kill his uncle Yukiie.

In the prior generation of Minamoto, Yoshitsune and Yoritomo's father had been the oldest brother. Legendary archer Uncle Tametomo was in the middle, and Uncle Yukiie was the youngest. At the beginning of the rebellion against the Taira, Uncle Yukiie had fought under Lord Kiso. But Yukiie had defected to Yoritomo's side just before the battle of Uji River. According to Kagetoki's son, Yoritomo now suspected Yukiie of treachery. So their uncle must die.

It is possible that Yoshitsune was still naive enough to believe that killing Yukiie would put him back in Yoritomo's good graces. More likely he realized this was Yoritomo's cynical way of using one threat to eliminate another. As soon as Yukiie was dead, Yoshitsune would be next.

Yoshitsune played for time. He told Kagetoki's son that Yukiie was no ordinary warrior who could be dispatched by underlings. Yoshitsune would have to kill Yukiie himself. He promised to carry out the task as soon as he recovered from his present illness.

Kagetoki's son returned to Kamakura. When he described Yoshitsune's appearance to his father and Yoritomo, Kagetoki suggested that Yoshitsune had simply not eaten for a few days in order to appear weak and had his skin burned just to look pathetic. "There is not the slightest doubt," Kagetoki claimed, "that he is acting in concert with Yukiie and making preparations [for rebellion]."

Yoritomo agreed. Obviously Yoshitsune must die. However, Yoritomo didn't want to send a large army to Kyoto. If he did, Yoshitsune would find out and mount a defense. What if Yoshitsune recruited a rebel force? What if he destroyed the rebuilt bridges at Uji and Seta and plunged the country into another civil war? Yoshitsune was the greatest general in Japanese history. Even commanding a small force, he was an enormous threat.

The lord of Kamakura needed an assassin.

The weather in Kyoto had cooled, and fall winds had stripped the trees of their leaves. Yoshitsune learned that one of Yoritomo's retainers, a warrior-monk named Tosabō Shōshun, had arrived in the city on a religious pilgrimage. Yoshitsune sent his friend Benkei, who was also a warrior-monk, to bring the man in for a chat.

When Shōshun arrived Yoshitsune asked, "Well? Have you no letter for me from Lord Yoritomo?"

Shōshun claimed Yoritomo didn't have anything to discuss with Yoshitsune. This was obviously not true—for one thing, Uncle Yukiie was still breathing—so Yoshitsune made the warrior-monk swear that he was not in Kyoto to do harm. Shōshun wrote out seven oaths on rice paper. Some he burned and swallowed; others he offered to a shrine.

Yoshitsune's lover, the dancer Shizuka, wasn't convinced. After Shōshun departed she sent two messenger boys to spy on the residence where the warrior-monk was staying. The boys didn't return. More worried than ever, Shizuka asked a serving woman to check on the boys. Night had fallen by the time the woman returned. When she heard what the servant had seen, Shizuka rushed to Yoshitsune.

The messenger boys lay dead—murdered at Shōshun's gate. Over eighty samurai in full armor crowded Shōshun's courtyard. Their horses stood saddled.

Yoshitsune's long months of worry and uncertainty vanished. If he had indeed been ill, he showed no sign of it that night. He leaped to his feet and called for his servants to alert his retainers. Fifty or so warriors, including Benkei and Tadanobu, were quartered in or near his residence. They would be seriously outnumbered by Shōshun's eighty men.

Shizuka tried to help Yoshitsune strap on his armor, but he drew his sword and ran outside to mount his warhorse with only the shoulder cord fastened. As soon as Benkei, Tadanobu, and Ise Saburō joined him in the courtyard, Yoshitsune ordered the outer gates thrown open. Hooves echoed in the dark as the assassins drew near.

Yoshitsune yelled a war cry and charged.

12

SHIZUKA'S SONG

Kyoto, Kamakura, and the Yoshino
Mountains, 1185–1186

Yoshitsune and his friends rode into the center of
Shōshun's band. Yoshitsune's other retainers, hastily
summoned from their nearby lodgings, attacked from the
sides. Clattering hooves, bellowing warriors, and whizzing
arrows turned the street into a dark and deadly battlefield.
Although they heavily outnumbered Yoshitsune's band,
Shōshun and his men were completely unprepared to
find themselves on the receiving end of a surprise assault.
Most of the would-be assassins died. The survivors broke
and fled.

Shōshun managed to slip away but made a fatal mis-
take: he tried to hide in the mountains north of Kyoto. It
seems that Yoshitsune was remembered fondly by those
who raised him, because the monks of Kurama tracked
Shōshun down. They dragged the warrior-monk back to
Kyoto and handed him to Yoshitsune.

"This is what you get for swearing all those oaths," Yoshitsune told Shōshun. Yoshitsune's companions marched the captive to the bank of the Kamo River and slashed off his head.

When your half brother sends assassins to kill you, it's a strong hint that your relationship is beyond repair. With all hope of reconciliation gone, Yoshitsune was forced to become the rebel Yoritomo imagined him to be.

He sought help from Go-Shirakawa by asking for an imperial mandate to attack Yoritomo. The Retired Emperor agreed. He may have sincerely wanted to help Yoshitsune. But divide and conquer had always been Go-Shirakawa's go-to strategy when dealing with troublesome samurai. Perhaps a Minamoto family feud would allow the imperial family to take back some of the power lost to the samurai lords.

It didn't take long for Yoritomo's spies to race back to Kamakura with shocking news: Yoshitsune was very much alive. Shōshun and most of his fellow assassins were very much dead. And Go-Shirakawa had just given Yoshitsune the sheriff's badge. Yoritomo was suddenly the outlaw.

Yoritomo leaped into action. With speed and energy more typical of Yoshitsune, the lord of Kamakura immediately demanded military service from his most important vassals. He knew some might be tempted to support Yoshitsune. But if he forced a decision now—without giving anyone the opportunity to contact Yoshitsune first—they would likely choose the safer course and stick with him. The lord of Kamakura ordered Kagetoki to send an advance strike force to Kyoto right away. Yoritomo promised to follow with a larger army as soon as one could be assembled.

Yoritomo also presented several horses to shrines as gifts, perhaps hoping that the gods would bless his half brother's destruction. The lord of Kamakura was always a devoutly religious man. Did he still wear that tiny statue of Kannon, the Buddhist goddess of mercy, tied in his hair? Did she nest there, silent and unnoticed?

Yoshitsune and Uncle Yukiie—the relative Yoritomo had ordered Yoshitsune to kill—suddenly discovered that they had more than a bloodline in common. The two agreed to join forces. Yet despite the imperial mandate Yoshitsune had received from the Retired Emperor, very few samurai lords were willing to join them. Many samurai were reluctant to cross the powerful lord of Kamakura. Most of all, however, they were exhausted by the civil war and ready for peace and stability. You know strife has gone on too long when even samurai are sick of violence.

On the third day of the eleventh month of 1185, just as the sun dawned, Yoshitsune and his uncle gathered their followers. It is said that Yoshitsune wore a red brocade robe over light-green armor. After all, honor demanded peacock-style gear. Benkei, Tadanobu, and Ise Saburō were with him. So was Shizuka.

News of Yoshitsune's rebellion had spread through Kyoto. Yoshitsune didn't have enough warriors to put up a fight for the city, but he certainly had enough warriors to pillage it. Everyone still had bad memories of Lord Kiso's rampage through the capital two years earlier. That morning parents whisked their children indoors. Charcoal sellers with blackened hands and beggars with twisted limbs disappeared from street corners; market stalls stood empty. Go-Shirakawa probably resigned himself to yet another kidnapping—standard operating procedure for desperate samurai lords. But it seems Yoshitsune valued something other than political gain, because the rebels rode quietly out of Kyoto.

Yoshitsune's band took the road leading southwest. They did not get far before a Yoritomo loyalist with a small group of samurai foolishly challenged them. Most of the loyalists died. Yoshitsune ordered their severed heads hung on trees as a gruesome offering to Hachiman, the Shinto god of war. It also served as a warning.

Three days later, Yoshitsune, his uncle Yukiie, and their followers reached a small port just a day's ride from Ichi-no-Tani. They planned to sail to Shikoku. Perhaps there, farther from Yoritomo's influence, Yoshitsune would be able to gather allies. They loaded their horses and piled into ships.

The vessels were already well out to sea when a fierce gale blew up from the west. Less than a year earlier, Yoshitsune had ridden a similar storm to victory at Yashima. But now the freezing wind drove his boats apart. Icy rain drenched the miserable, frightened passengers. As the tempest grew, so did the waves, towering beasts of water able to swallow men, women, horses, and boats in a single gulp.

Afterward, storytellers claimed that the vengeful souls of Taira drowned at Dan-no-Ura had stirred the violent storm. They credited Benkei for saving Yoshitsune's life: when all seemed lost, the storytellers said, the warrior-monk climbed into the prow of Yoshitsune's boat and loosed arrows to drive away the sinister clouds.

When the wind calmed (and the Taira ghosts presumably departed), Yoshitsune's battered vessel struggled to the nearest beach. Yoshitsune, his closest friends, and Shizuka were among the few survivors. Most of Yoshitsune's samurai and all his hopes drowned off the Settsu coast. Without at least a small band, Yoshitsune couldn't present himself to other samurai lords as a credible alternative to Yoritomo. Hiding now offered his best chance of survival. If he waited, the situation might change. Others might rise against Yoritomo, or Yoritomo might die.

By chance Uncle Yukiie's boat also reached shore. He parted from Yoshitsune and left to seek refuge with friends. Yukiie's freedom lasted only a few months before he was tracked down and murdered by Yoritomo's retainers.

Benkei, Shizuka, and Yoshitsune took shelter at a nearby temple. Yoshitsune's surviving companions probably also included Tadanobu, his old friend from Hiraizumi; Ise Saburō, the former bandit; and Washinoo, the young hunter who had guided Yoshitsune to the top of the cliffs at Ichi-no-Tani.

Yoshitsune asked Shizuka to wait at the temple. He and his samurai disappeared. A few days later one of Yoshitsune's men arrived with a horse and a message for Shizuka: she was to rejoin Yoshitsune at his hiding place deep in the snowy wilds of the Yoshino Mountains.

The lovers spent five days together. Storytellers later said that "when Yoshitsune summoned his resolution, Shizuka could not bear to leave, and when Shizuka steeled herself to go, Yoshitsune's courage failed." Finally Yoshitsune told her she must return to Kyoto. Perhaps he believed that Shizuka's fame would protect her from Yoritomo's vengeance.

We don't know if Shizuka told Yoshitsune that she was carrying his child.

Yoritomo gathered an army and led it out of Kamakura. Before he reached Kyoto, messengers arrived with the news of Yoshitsune's flight from the capital. The lord of Kamakura promptly turned around and headed home.

Rumors flew. Some said that Yoshitsune and Yukiie had drowned off the Settsu coast. Yoritomo wanted to make sure. Local samurai were ordered to "search the mountains and forests, rivers and marshes, and to deliver up their bodies at an early date."

The lord of Kamakura relished the news of the terrible storm. He smugly claimed that heaven itself had punished Yoshitsune. However, Yoritomo didn't intend to leave all the punishing to ghosts and gods. He let it be known that "as there are monks . . . among Yoshitsune's partisans, they too shall be sought out and removed," a threat probably targeted at the monks of Kurama Temple, Yoshitsune's boyhood home. The lord of Kamakura also confiscated all property belonging to Yoshitsune's father-in-law, even though the man was Yoritomo's own retainer and had married his daughter to Yoshitsune at Yoritomo's request.

The lord of Kamakura was furious with Go-Shirakawa for signing the proclamation naming him an enemy of the state. One of Go-Shirakawa's ministers tried to claim that Yoshitsune had bullied the Retired Emperor into signing the edict, adding that Yoshitsune's rebellion "was undoubtedly the work of the devil."

Yoritomo tartly replied, "So long as the throne does not authorize the seizure of Yukiie and Yoshitsune, there will be chaos in the provinces and the people will be destroyed. Thus the great devil in Japan must be some other devil than the one mentioned."

Go-Shirakawa got the hint. He hastily signed a new imperial edict naming Yoshitsune public enemy number one. And at Yoritomo's request he stripped land and titles from all samurai and aristocrats known to be Yoshitsune's friends.

Reports continued to pour into Kamakura. Maybe Yoshitsune hadn't drowned after all; some of the boats had reached shore. Yoritomo used the rumors of Yoshitsune's survival as an excuse to station his own retainers throughout Japan, particularly in areas where his control was still incomplete. Yoritomo's retainers would oversee the immense manhunt for Yoshitsune. They were allowed to "seize and use horses from manors, irrespective of their ownership by powerful officials and influential families" and to help themselves to whatever provisions they needed.

To fund his new police force, Yoritomo forced Go-Shirakawa to impose a special rice tax on all land, even land belonging to the imperial family and other nobles. The lord of Kamakura was already Japan's supreme military commander. He now increased his influence over taxes and became Japan's top cop. It did not take long for the lord of Kamakura's wide net to snare its first victim. Eleven days after the disastrous storm that wrecked Yoshitsune's hopes, Yoritomo's men captured Shizuka.

Before their parting Yoshitsune gave Shizuka gold and silver and ordered servants to escort her to Kyoto. The servants promptly stole Shizuka's horse and money and disappeared. Shizuka wandered downhill in hopes of finding shelter before the cold killed her. Storytellers later claimed that "blood from her bruised feet reddened the snow of the Yoshino Mountains, freezing water dripped from her tear-drenched sleeves, and ice formed on the hem of her skirts, weighting her body so that she could scarcely move." Almost twenty-six years earlier, Yoshitsune's mother, Tokiwa, had staggered through snowdrifts with Yoshitsune bundled in her arms, fleeing a samurai lord bent on her children's destruction. Now Shizuka, lost and abandoned, trudged through the wilderness under winter stars, carrying Yoshitsune's baby in her womb.

At last Shizuka stumbled upon a mountain temple. The monks, who thought she appeared "strange and eerie," turned her over to Yoritomo's men. Under questioning she revealed that she and Yoshitsune had parted in the Yoshino Mountains. Yoritomo ordered the search in the region redoubled. After several months' captivity in Kyoto, Shizuka was taken to Kamakura. By the time she reached Yoritomo's headquarters, her pregnancy was obvious. It was just as obvious that the lord of Kamakura would never allow a son of Yoshitsune's to live. Shizuka could only pray for a girl.

Shizuka's presence excited the Kamakura elite. Compared to Kyoto, Kamakura was a small town and a cultural backwater. Everyone knew of Shizuka's beauty and divine talents; Yoritomo's senior retainers and their wives hungered for a glimpse. Possibly Yoritomo was also curious. And perhaps he could not resist an opportunity to injure

Yoshitsune from afar. Whatever his motive, the lord of Kamakura ordered Shizuka to dance.

Shizuka tried to plead ill health. She was, after all, seven or eight months pregnant. Yoritomo insisted. He told her she would dedicate her dance to Hachiman, the Shinto god of war and patron god of the Minamoto. Shizuka would also pray for the success of Yoritomo's government.

The reed-thatched shrine dedicated to Hachiman stood on a hill overlooking Yoritomo's ever-expanding city. Under a roofed, open-air hall on the temple grounds, Yoritomo's servants arranged a raised dance platform draped in Chinese damasks and airy fabrics. On the day of the performance, Yoritomo, his senior retainers, and their families settled on viewing platforms with translucent blinds that offered the women a semblance of privacy. The men wore small, stiff caps, silk jackets, and starched wide-legged trousers. The women's floor-length hair spilled down the back of their voluminous robes.

Kagetoki attended, as well as Yoritomo's father-in-law. Both had betrayed their former Taira masters to become Yoritomo's closest confidants. For a man obsessed with his half brother's supposed disloyalty, the lord of Kamakura was curiously comfortable in the company of traitors.

It is said that Shizuka, wearing a white under-robe and white wide-legged trousers, was carried in on a litter. She stepped out, bowed, and prayed to Hachiman. The patron god of the Minamoto didn't belong just to Yoritomo. He belonged to Yoshitsune and their unborn child, too.

Shizuka began with a popular and well-known song. Later, storytellers said "the amazed and delighted spectators of all degrees caught their breath and praised her until the clouds rang."

What Shizuka did next was as brave as anything Yoshitsune ever did—possibly braver. Nineteen-year-old Shizuka carried no weapons, wore no armor, and had no horse to carry her to safety. Not a single friend stood by her side. She was heavy with child and as vulnerable as any woman can possibly be. Yet on that spring day in 1186, this young woman danced before Yoritomo, the most pitiless man in Japan, and sang this song:

Would that I could somehow
Make yesterday today.
How I long for him—
The person who vanished,
Cleaving a way
Through the white snows
On Yoshino's peaks.
He has vanished utterly—
The person who disappeared,
Cleaving a way
Through the white snows
On Yoshino's peaks.

Yoritomo was furious. His wife tried to convince him that Shizuka was a loyal woman and as such should be commended. Yoritomo managed to control his anger long enough to lift his blind and shove out a silk robe—the standard payment for a performer.

Afterward, it is said, Yoritomo wanted to rip open Shizuka's belly and kill her child then and there. Even Yoshitsune's mortal enemy Kagetoki thought this was a tad extreme. He counseled Yoritomo to wait a few months. If Shizuka delivered a boy, the baby would be murdered. If Shizuka delivered a girl, the baby would be taken away from her and raised to be a maid in Yoritomo's household.

As Shizuka awaited their child's birth, the hunt for Yoshi-tsune continued. Yoritomo's men searched the length and breadth of western, central, and eastern Japan for the famous fugitive. Yet despite the odds against him, our man didn't give up. He got creative. As quietly and softly as an evening snowfall, Yoshitsune disappeared.

13

THE FUGITIVE

LOCATIONS UNKNOWN, 1185–1187

Little is known of Yoshitsune's whereabouts from the winter of 1185 through the spring of 1187. During this time Yoshitsune and his companions probably moved through the mountainous regions of central Japan. Most people avoided the mountains because bandits and demons lurked there.

Yoshitsune and his men disguised themselves as *yamabushi*. These wandering monks sought magical powers through feats of iron endurance, meditating for hours under freezing waterfalls and racing up steep peaks. They were holy men who sought the sacred among living cedars rather than wooden temples. Since yamabushi also practiced the martial arts, Yoshitsune and his friends could carry weapons without raising suspicion. And most important, traveling monks were usually waved through government checkpoints.

Yoshitsune and his friends were oddly well prepared for their new life. Benkei really *was* a monk, after all, and Yoshitsune had trained to become one. Ise Saburō was a former mountain bandit, and Washinoo was a mountain hunter.

Unfortunately, their exile began in winter. Waterproof fabrics, down padding, and wool were unknown in twelfth-century Japan. The disguised fugitives probably wore clothing made of woven hemp, straw snow boots, and straw cloaks. A traveler wearing one of these bushy coats looked like a thatched hut with legs.

That Yoshitsune and his friends survived at all is a testament to their physical toughness, their ability to think on their feet, and their knack for knowing whom to trust. Many people helped them on the sly. Yes, Yoritomo was the most powerful samurai in Japan and Yoshitsune was officially a traitor and a rebel. But many people admired Yoshitsune. They held their own quiet opinions about which brother had suffered betrayal.

Those who actually knew Yoshitsune's whereabouts kept silent. But other people couldn't stop talking. The hero of Uji River, Ichi-no-Tani, Yashima, and Dan-no-Ura—now a criminal! Yoritomo's nationwide manhunt spread Yoshitsune's fame across Japan. People hungered for the latest news. Where was Yoshitsune hiding? How had he and his friends outwitted their pursuers? Forget Great-Grandfather Yoshiie the barbarian-killer and Uncle Tametomo the famous archer; now people begged for stories about Yoshitsune and his faithful friends. Into the void of actual information, many storytellers—both of Yoshitsune's time and later ages—poured their imaginations.

A tale was told about Tadanobu, brother of the fallen Tsuginobu. In this story Yoshitsune and seventeen companions had just left Shizuka behind and hadn't had time to adopt their yamabushi disguise. As they trudged through the Yoshino Mountains, they spotted enemy warrior-monks approaching.

"Let me delay the monks with arrows while you escape," Tadanobu suggested.

Yoshitsune refused. But Benkei advised him to say good-bye to Tadanobu "with a good grace."

Yoshitsune reluctantly agreed, but said, "When you become tired, you will find your present sword too long. A long sword is a handicap to an exhausted man." He took Tadanobu's sword and gave him a shorter, gold-mounted blade. "This weapon, which has been as precious as life to me, I give to you now that you are exchanging your life for mine."

Tadanobu dressed in Yoshitsune's fine armor and silver helmet; Yoshitsune put on Tadanobu's plainer set. The two old friends said good-bye.

As the warrior-monks drew near, they spotted Tadanobu in his flashy armor. Thinking they had cornered Yoshitsune, they charged uphill. Tadanobu ducked through the trees and circled behind them, shooting arrows and bellowing out orders to Benkei, Ise Saburō, and Washinoo, as if those men were also hidden in the woods. The attackers sent most of their arrows flying toward these imaginary threats. A huge warrior-monk called out, demanding that "Yoshitsune" meet him in single combat. Tadanobu obliged.

The two exchanged arrows and clashed in a sword fight. Then—in a sequence that shouts "action movie!"—

Tadanobu toppled off a cliff, followed by the warrior-monk. When they landed on a ledge, the furious sword fight continued. Tadanobu killed the warrior-monk and threw the man's severed head to his companions. The rest of the warrior-monks fled in terror.

Tadanobu followed the monks back to their temple. His fight had left him famished, so he broke in, wolfed down the monks' food, and guzzled their *sake* (rice wine). After dining, Tadanobu calmly set fire to the building. He strolled onto a veranda to shout insults at the warrior-monks, pretended to stab himself, and retreated back inside. He secretly escaped the fire by punching a hole in the roof of the flaming building and leaping to the steep hillside behind. After discarding Yoshitsune's conspicuous armor, Tadanobu sauntered back into Kyoto.

Meanwhile (or so the story goes), Yoshitsune and his remaining sixteen followers made their escape. But the deep snow made it impossible for them to cover their tracks. The warrior-monks, swarming like angry bees after the Tadanobu incident, once again picked up the fugitives' trail.

As he waded through the snow, Yoshitsune heard faint voices. Looking back, he saw 150 enemy monks threading their way up the cedar-covered hill. Yoshitsune led his men deeper into the mountains—only to find their path blocked by a cascading waterfall. Frothy water tumbled between walls of rock covered by snow and ice.

Benkei and Yoshitsune spied a possible crossing downstream where the river sped through a channel between two high banks. Three tall bamboos stood on the opposite side, so weighted by frost that their tips curved out over the water. Holding up the skirt panels of his armor to free his legs, Yoshitsune lowered his head and leaped toward the bamboo. By grasping the bamboo stalks, he managed to pull himself onto the opposite bank.

Yoshitsune urged the others to follow. "It's much easier than it looks from there. Come on, all of you."

Ise Saburō, Washinoo, and thirteen others made the leap. Only Benkei remained. But instead of crossing at the easiest spot, the warrior-monk walked upstream. He swept the snow from a rocky ledge jutting over the water.

"It was disgusting to watch you men holding on to those bamboo stalks and making such a fuss about crossing a mountain stream," Benkei shouted. "Get out of the way while I show you how easy it is to jump across."

Yoshitsune made a point of bending over to lash his snow boots tighter. "Don't pay any attention to him," he told the others.

Benkei jumped—but not quite far enough. He gave a desperate cry as he tumbled into the river, bouncing off rock after rock as the icy water swept him downstream. Yoshitsune grabbed a kumade, ran to the riverbank, and just managed to snag the back of his friend's armor with the iron claw. Ise Saburō helped him pull Benkei ashore.

"Your legs aren't as clever as your tongue," Yoshitsune said.

"Everyone makes mistakes," Benkei responded cheerfully.

Benkei strolled back to the bamboo hanging over the river. He slashed the stalks off and reburied the ends in the snow. Then he, Yoshitsune, and the rest hid nearby. They readied their bows.

The enemy warrior-monks followed the bootprints in the snow straight to the river crossing. Two warrior-monks leaped, just catching the tips of the bamboo. The severed stalks flew out of the snowbank and the monks splashed backward into the tumbling river. After watching their companions disappear downstream, none of the other warrior-monks had the courage to cross.

As their enemies trudged away in defeat, one of Yoshitsune's men shot a humming-bulb arrow over their heads. Just to rub it in.

The most famous tale about Yoshitsune's fugitive days involved an attempt to pass through a government checkpoint. A samurai named Togashi commanded a barrier complete with archer's towers, standing shields, and an impenetrable wall of brambles.

Benkei greeted Togashi. He told him that they were yamabushi seeking donations for a temple at Nara, a religious center south of Kyoto.

Togashi asked Benkei to read his "subscription list." Monks collecting donations usually carried these scrolls boasting of their temple's illustrious history. Reading the subscription list aloud to prospective donors was the twelfth-century equivalent of a TV commercial.

Benkei didn't have a subscription list. But he did have a scroll, so he pulled it out. In his deep, rich voice, he pretended to read a "history" that he invented on the spot.

Satisfied, Togashi waved them through. But as they passed, the samurai caught a glimpse of Yoshitsune. That day Yoshitsune was disguised as a baggage carrier, apparently in the hopes that no one would give the lowest-ranking member of the group a second glace. But Togashi thought he looked like the famous fugitive and said so. He ordered the travelers to halt.

"So he looks like Yoshitsune, does he?" Benkei strolled over. "That's something this rascal of a porter can remember for the rest of his life."

Benkei turned to Yoshitsune and berated him for lagging behind and causing trouble. "It's been one thing after another with you lately. Here, how do you like this?" He snatched a staff from Yoshitsune's hand and beat him mercilessly. Togashi, convinced of his error—no retainer of the *real* Yoshitsune would abuse his master so!—let them pass.

Afterward Benkei tearfully apologized. Yoshitsune assured him that he wasn't to blame.

The miseries of most unhappy families are private, but the miseries of the Minamoto family kept all of Japan in an uproar. Yoritomo's men arrested anyone suspected of aiding Yoshitsune. The head monk of Kurama and a former teacher of Yoshitsune's were sent to Kamakura for questioning. Yoshitsune's mother, Tokiwa, was interrogated. Eventually Yoritomo's men caught one of Yoshitsune's servants and tried to pry information from him. They still couldn't catch Yoshitsune.

But Yoritomo did have Shizuka. He kept her under guard in a seaside house near Kamakura. About a month after her performance at the Hachiman shrine, Shizuka's labor pains began. In those days a midwife attended the mother-to-be. Others took care of spiritual needs: one holy man read religious texts while another purified the birthplace.

Someone else twanged a bowstring to ward off evil spirits. During the birth of Shizuka's child, evil was clearly present, though not in a spiritual form. Yoritomo's men waited outside like vultures.

Nineteen-year-old Shizuka gave birth, in pain and sorrow, to a little boy. Yoritomo's men carried the baby to the sea and drowned him in the waves. Afterward Shizuka was allowed to retire to a Buddhist nunnery. It is said that she died there in autumn of the following year, unable to bear the agony of her memories.

Yoritomo's manhunt eventually snared Tadanobu. In the ninth month of 1186, Yoshitsune's oldest friend snuck into Kyoto to visit a married woman with whom he was having a love affair. Perhaps motivated by thoughts of reward, the woman told her husband, who informed one of Yoritomo's men. Yoritomo's retainer gathered a large force of samurai before attacking. He later reported to the lord of Kamakura: "Tadanobu, being naturally a tough soldier, fought back and could not be easily subdued." But in the end Tadanobu fell.

Yet Yoshitsune remained a free man. Finally, in early 1187, a rumor swept through Kyoto: Yoshitsune was dead! The famous fugitive had killed himself at a remote mountain temple.

Yoritomo rejoiced . . . until he discovered that it was all a lie. We know that at about this time Yoshitsune and his friends left central Japan, so perhaps it was Yoshitsune himself who had started the rumor. If Yoritomo's men thought Yoshitsune was dead, they might relax their vigilance enough to allow the fugitives to slip through.

Yoshitsune and his band did indeed get past the checkpoints. The true adventures of their hazardous journey are lost, yet in danger and daring probably exceeded anything a storyteller could dream up. All we know is that sometime in the spring of 1187, Yoshitsune led his last faithful friends to the only place where they might find solace and refuge.

14

FEAST OF ARROWS

HIRAIZUMI, 1187–1189

Some things hadn't changed. Hiraizumi was as elegant as ever. The bustling city remained a magnet for painters, calligraphers, sculptors, lacquerers, and metalsmiths. Lavish temples still graced the hilltops, and the doors of Hidehira's mansion still opened to gardens of heavenly perfection.

Yoshitsune arrived in the fourth or fifth month of 1187, once again in disguise and once again hunted by a powerful samurai lord. But the brave teenager who had asked for sanctuary thirteen years before was now twenty-eight. He was the most famous (or notorious) samurai in Japan, a man who had conquered all and lost all. Once again old man Hidehira welcomed him.

The lord of Hiraizumi gave his foster son a residence on a ridge overlooking the Koromo River, not far from

Hidehira's own compound. Since Yoshitsune no doubt arrived with nothing but his weapons and the clothes on his back, Hidehira's generosity probably included horses, armor, silk clothing, and servants—everything suited to a samurai of Yoshitsune's birth and distinction.

We know that one of Yoshitsune's wives joined him in exile, along with a daughter born sometime during 1186. We don't know which wife—the daughter of Yoritomo's retainer or the daughter of the Taira captive? Nor is it known how Yoshitsune's wife and child evaded Yoritomo and reached Hiraizumi.

For two seasons Yoshitsune lived in peace. We can imagine him enjoying the lovely distraction of his daughter at play as cicadas buzzed in the sultry summer air. In the cooler evenings he may have rested on the veranda with his wife to watch the Koromo River flow smoothly by. With Benkei, Ise Saburō, and Washinoo, he may have played dice, *go*, or backgammon as they shared memories of their battles and narrow escapes. Many of those memories surely involved Tsuginobu and Tadanobu, the loyal brothers from Hiraizumi who had not lived to see their homeland again.

Frequent invitations probably arrived from Hidehira. The men in the family loved to gallop off in search of deer and boar. In the fall, when the grass turned golden, they rode into the fields and marshes with goshawks on their wrists and sent the fierce birds winging after pheasants and geese. Feasts and entertainment surely followed. Hidehira's wealth attracted the finest singers, dancers, and musicians. Though perhaps a shirabyōshi performance was too painful for Yoshitsune to endure.

Yoshitsune's small circle of friends certainly loved him. Did he notice that not one of them was a Minamoto?

The days shortened and cooled. On the ridge where Yoshitsune's house stood, wind rushed through the trees like a river in flood.

Even Hiraizumi wasn't safe from the lord of Kamakura. Yoritomo could now demand military service from all the samurai who had pledged loyalty during the Taira-Minamoto conflict, and he could pay for war by levying new taxes. Yoshitsune's victories had helped make Yoritomo the most powerful samurai lord in Japan. Now that samurai lord wanted Hidehira's golden kingdom.

Letters arrived from Kamakura ordering Hidehira to give up Yoshitsune. Of course, messengers took weeks to go back and forth between Kamakura and Hiraizumi, and Hidehira was a master at using the time lag to his advantage. He hemmed and hawed and stalled. But the excuses had barely begun to flow when Hidehira fell ill.

The lord of Hiraizumi called his sons to his deathbed. He declared Yasuhira, a son in his early thirties, to be his heir and the next head of the Hiraizumi Fujiwara. He ordered Tadahira, a son probably close in age to Yoshitsune, to support his older brother. But Hidehira named Yoshitsune, rather than one of his sons, commander-in-chief of Hiraizumi's warriors. Hidehira probably guessed that only a commander of Yoshitsune's brilliance and experience could save Hiraizumi if Yoritomo sent an army north. Yet the old man's last request may have fatally fractured whatever relationship existed between Yoshitsune and his foster brother Yasuhira.

The lord of Hiraizumi died on the twenty-ninth day of the tenth month of 1187. After the funeral Hidehira's family discussed his last instructions. Tadahira, the younger son, spoke in Yoshitsune's favor: the family should honor Hidehira's wishes. But his older brother Yasuhira steadfastly refused to turn any authority over to Yoshitsune. Hiraizumi's warriors would remain under his control.

Without a strong samurai force, Yoshitsune couldn't protect his adopted land. He couldn't protect himself, either. And he had nowhere else to go.

For several months winter snows discouraged travel in and out of Hiraizumi. But by spring 1188, senior officers from the imperial court arrived in the north. They carried orders signed by Retired Emperor Go-Shirakawa (written at Yoritomo's insistence) requiring Yasuhira to arrest Yoshitsune. Although he feared Yoritomo, Yasuhira still resisted. He may have been playing for time, or he may have found it difficult to betray his foster brother. Or both.

Spring passed into summer. That fall another set of courtiers arrived carrying even more strongly worded orders from Go-Shirakawa: the fugitive Yoshitsune *must* be given up. Yasuhira was also named as Yoshitsune's co-conspirator.

Meanwhile, spies scurried back and forth between Kamakura and Hiraizumi. Yoritomo's spies told him about Yasuhira's shaky loyalty to Yoshitsune. Yasuhira's spies reported that Kamakura was preparing a massive military campaign.

Yoritomo sent letters to Yasuhira promising to call off military action if Yasuhira took action against Yoshitsune. Refusal meant war.

Yoshitsune was living quietly in his residence above the Koromo River, well aware that his foster brother might betray him at any moment. Preparations must be made: sharp swords, makeshift shields, stockpiles of arrows, and constant vigilance. His home stood on a ridge that offered a clear view of any who might approach. The grand master of the sneak attack would not be caught unawares.

Certainly Yoshitsune had ample time to consider the manner of his death. He no doubt wanted a last stand that would be equal to the rest of his life—defiant, dignified, and irresistibly courageous. Yoshitsune had lived better than most and probably wanted to die better, too, seizing one final moment of glory.

In those days the Japanese elite cultivated a sense that is now called *mono no aware*: the poignant awareness of beauty that cannot last. In those last months Yoshitsune lived mono no aware. There was no telling which cup of sake might be the last to be enjoyed or which story might be the last to be shared. Every kiss became a final embrace.

On the thirtieth day of the fourth month of 1189, several hundred of Yasuhira's warriors rode up the ridge toward Yoshitsune's residence. Although the result is briefly recorded in the annals of Yoritomo's government, the details remain a mystery. It did not take long, however, for people to fill the gaps with things rumored or imagined. This is the story that has been told.

When the death squad approached, Yoshitsune's ten remaining companions—including Benkei, Ise Saburō, and Washinoo—rushed inside to report that Yasuhira wasn't among them. Instead of leading the attack himself, he had given command to one of his retainers. This was crucial information to Yoshitsune: it told him none of the attackers was high-ranking enough to be a worthy opponent. Pride mattered to the bitter end.

Yoshitsune's friends hurried back outside. Two men

stationed themselves on the roof, using window shutters torn from the building as shields. Ise Saburō, Washinoo, Benkei, and five others took positions near the front gate.

Benkei jumped onto an elevated plank. He dressed well for his last battle: black armor decorated with small gilded butterflies. As Yasuhira's assassins rode to the residence overlooking the Koromo River, the warrior-monk danced a jig and bellowed a song:

> *How delightful are the waters of the cataract—*
> *How pleasant the sound of the cataract's waters,*
> *Never ceasing in the driest of weather!*
> *Sing on, sing on!*
> *Ah, the armor and helmets of the eastern rabble—*
> *Heads and all, they are cut off,*
> *Tossed into the Koromo River*
> *And carried away!*

The samurai stationed on the roof sent arrows zinging down as Benkei, Ise Saburō, Washinoo, and the rest defended the gate with swords and naginata. Only a few enemy horsemen at a time could charge into the narrow opening, so at first Yoshitsune's men were able to hold off the attackers. But eventually Benkei was wounded in the throat. Though blood dripped down the plates of his armor, he continued to fight furiously.

"That monk is crazy," one enemy remarked.

"Stay away from him," warned another. "There's no telling what he'll do."

No matter how brave the heart, arms tire. Feet slow and falter. First Washinoo the hunter died, after killing five enemies, then the former bandit Ise Saburō, who left nine of Yasuhira's samurai lying in the dirt. One of Yoshitsune's archers toppled from the roof with an arrow in his neck.

Benkei rushed inside to say his last words to Yoshitsune. The friends believed that their wandering souls would meet again while awaiting rebirth. Not even death could sever their bond. "Wait for me, my lord," Benkei said, "where the road to hell branches off."

"Join me in the next world," Yoshitsune replied.

Benkei returned to the fight, charging into his enemies as if possessed by a demon. With a sword in one hand and a naginata in the other, Benkei slashed horses' bellies, knocked riders into the dirt, and lopped off their heads. Cautious warriors pulled back and pelted the warrior-monk with arrows.

The attackers withdrew for a moment to regroup. Benkei stabbed his naginata into the ground and leaned upon it. His enemies could not quite believe he remained on his feet; the warrior-monk was so bristled with arrows that he looked like a porcupine. Still, no one was anxious to fight him.

At last one of Yasuhira's warriors rode cautiously past. The swish of wind from the galloping horse tipped Benkei's corpse into the dust. The warrior-monk had died on his feet, defending Yoshitsune to the end.

As his friends fought and died outside, Yoshitsune gathered his wife, his daughter, and one retainer in a Buddhist altar room. The decision had been made. The tool selected and sharpened. The only thing left was the awareness of the moment: the sound of the battle outside, the smell of the incense on the altar, the sight of the peaceful face on the statue of Buddha.

And the act itself.

Yoshitsune used a six-inch knife. What were his thoughts in that moment before the fatal cut? Did his mind fix on Uncle Tametomo, who had died in a similar fashion? Perhaps he thought only of those who had loved him most: Hidehira, the warrior brothers Tsuginobu and Tadanobu, Benkei, Ise Saburō, Washinoo, Shizuka, his wife, and his daughter.

The knife pierced flesh. Pain erased thought. Yoshitsune leaned heavily on an armrest, slowly bleeding to death.

When Yasuhira's men had first appeared, Yoshitsune had begged his wife to escape with their child. He told her Hidehira's widow would treat them well and send them back to Kyoto. But his wife had staunchly refused. In samurai families, self-destruction was not limited to the men.

Now Yoshitsune's retainer argued with Yoshitsune's wife. She steadfastly insisted that she and her daughter must follow Yoshitsune in death. They, too, hoped to join him in the next world.

The horrified retainer wept uncontrollably as he killed Yoshitsune's wife. The little girl died with a single piteous cry.

Yoshitsune's eyes fluttered open. "My wife?"

"She lies dead by your side." The retainer told him that the child was gone, too.

Yoshitsune was fading fast; he could no longer see. Unconsciousness was almost upon him. Feebly he touched the bodies.

It was almost time to let go. Almost. It would be so much easier to retreat from the unbearable pain. So much easier to fade away. So much easier to give in. But if the attackers found his body . . .

One last task. One final defiance. One way to deny his enemies his head.

Drawing his last breath, Yoshitsune gasped: "Quickly, quickly, set fire to the house."

Epilogue

THE SAMURAI WEEPS

Storytellers claimed that Yoshitsune ordered his mansion set on fire. If that did happen, Yasuhira's men apparently broke in before the flames spread. Yoshitsune's attempt to keep his body in one piece failed. The attackers cut off his head and placed it in a black-lacquered tub full of sake to preserve it. A messenger carried the tub to Koshigoe, the small town outside Kamakura where Yoshitsune had once waited in vain for a reunion with Yoritomo.

Yoritomo sent Kagetoki to confirm the identity of the gruesome offering. Even Kagetoki wept, it is said, when Yoshitsune's head was pulled from the tub. But perhaps he cried crocodile tears.

Yoritomo's promise to spare Hiraizumi was a lie. In the seventh month of 1189—three months after Yoshitsune's death—Yoritomo headed north with the largest army ever assembled in Japan. Yoritomo used his punitive expedition against Hiraizumi as a way of testing his vassals' loyalty. If anyone refused to join his war party, they might lose their land rights or face execution.

Yasuhira's warriors met the Minamoto army at a fortified site south of Hiraizumi. They fought for three days before being overwhelmed. Yasuhira fled north, pausing to destroy his city before its riches could be claimed by Yoritomo. On that dark day "the treasures of three generations" vanished.

The lord of Kamakura entered Hiraizumi on a rainy autumn evening. He found a deserted city already reduced to ashes. Yoritomo's men combed the ruins of Hidehira's once-splendid mansion and found a few small treasures that escaped the flames: a crane made of gold, a cat made of silver, flutes carved from ivory, and lamps made of lapis lazuli. Hiraizumi, the jewel of Japan, never recovered. Today only the Hall of Gold and one small library are left to remind us of its former glory.

Yasuhira, the new lord of Hiraizumi and betrayer of Yoshitsune, did not fare well. A disloyal retainer murdered him and packed his head off to Yoritomo. Tadahira, the foster brother who had always remained loyal to Yoshitsune, was already dead. Yasuhira had assassinated him, possibly because of his staunch support of Yoshitsune.

Later that year Yoritomo built a temple in Kamakura where pacification prayers were offered to the spirits of Yoshitsune and the dead lords of Hiraizumi. It seems he feared vengeful ghosts.

On the seventh day of the eleventh month of 1190, Yoritomo finally visited Kyoto. It was the first time he had set foot in the capital since being carted away as Kiyomori's captive thirty years before. The lord of Kamakura paraded into the city with one thousand Minamoto warriors as his honor guard. He rode a black horse and wore a flap of deer hide over a glossy robe of dark blue, sky blue, and red. Like a dog lifting his leg to mark another dog's territory, Yoritomo built a residence smack on the foundations of Kiyomori's old home. Kamakura, however, always remained his headquarters.

Two years later, sixty-five-year-old Retired Emperor Go-Shirakawa died after a lingering illness. Despite losing most of his power, he had always stubbornly refused to give Yoritomo the rank of *shogun* (military leader of Japan). The next head of the imperial family was more of a pushover. In 1192 Yoritomo received the honor.

Yoritomo and Yoshitsune's other half brother, Noriyori, tried his best to stay on Yoritomo's good side. Unfortunately Yoritomo didn't really have a good side. He assassinated Noriyori in 1193.

In 1199 Yoritomo was out riding when his horse suddenly spooked and threw him to the ground. He died soon after from his injuries. People later claimed that the ghosts of Yoshitsune and little Emperor Antoku (odd teammates, all things considered) had frightened Yoritomo's horse.

Yoritomo was survived by two sons. According to his instructions, his right-hand man, Kagetoki, was supposed to act as guardian for Yoritomo's seventeen-year-old heir, Yoriie, in the event of Yoritomo's death. But Yoriie apparently detested Kagetoki as much as everyone else did. He had Kagetoki murdered in 1200 along with Kagetoki's entire family and all of his closest retainers.

The Minamoto family seemed possessed by murderous urges. Yoriie was strangled in 1204—possibly with the approval of his own mother after he allied with factions she opposed. His younger brother Sanetomo then became shogun. Sanetomo excelled as a poet but lacked political skills and eventually became a liability. In 1219 Yoriie's mentally ill son beheaded his uncle Sanetomo on the steps of the Hachiman shrine in Kamakura. Yoriie's son was quickly executed for the murder, possibly to cover up the involvement of other members of his family.

Minamoto rule of Japan ended on this fratricidal note. If Yoritomo had left a strong and loyal brother alive to protect his heirs, would history have turned out differently?

After the deaths of Yoritomo's sons and grandson, the people who seized control of Japan were Yoritomo's widow, Hōjō Masako; her father, Hōjō Tokimasa; and her brother, Hōjō Yoshitoki.

The Hōjō family was—wait for it!—a minor branch of the Taira.

Although Yoritomo and Yoshitsune's line died out, the world they created endured. The aristocratic Heian age ended in 1185, the year of Yoshitsune's victory at Dan-no-Ura and the expansion of Yoritomo's power and influence. Samurai rule of Japan lasted until 1868—almost seven hundred years.

In the years following Yoritomo's rule, a succession of shogun continued to chip away at the wealth and influence of the court nobility. Kyoto's poetic culture faded. By 1500 the imperial family was so poor it couldn't afford to pay for the new emperor's enthronement ceremony. Ironically, the samurai never lost their admiration for the aristocratic world they destroyed. Fine artistic sensibility became part of the warrior way and was expressed in new cultural practices ranging from the gentle tea ceremony to the appalling and intricately ritualized act of seppuku.

The rise of the samurai also changed Japanese literature. As soon as time had decomposed bodies and dulled memories, the cataclysmic civil war became glorious. The Japanese wanted to remember the saga of the Taira and the Minamoto and, by remembering, honor and soothe the spirits of the fallen warriors. This homage to the dead was most notably achieved in a war chronicle called *The Tale of the Heike*. It gave Yoshitsune immortality.

The first versions of the *Heike* ("Heike" is an alternative reading of the Chinese characters for "Taira family") were compiled between 1198 and 1221, when eyewitnesses to the events were still alive. The first compiler was said to be a monk named Yukinaga who "wrote with a detailed knowledge of [Junior Lieutenant] Yoshitsune's activities." The most well-known version of the *Heike* was composed in 1371 by Kakuichi, a blind monk, and sung to medieval Japanese audiences of all social classes.

If many aspects of Yoshitsune's life fit our idealized notions about the Japanese warrior—fierce loyalty, honor above self-preservation, reckless bravery, courage in the face of death, the iconic role of ritual suicide—it is because he is one of the most prominent historical figures in the *Heike*. Generation after generation of Japanese read or listened to the *Heike* and took its lessons to heart. Yoshitsune, the brilliant commander, was remembered as the standard against which all other men were measured. For almost seven hundred years, samurai navigated by him as if he were a fixed star.

Of course, the warrior ideals modeled by Yoshitsune

were difficult to live up to. In truth, many later samurai engaged in the same backstabbing, self-serving behavior that is the dark side of *Heike* and other twelfth-century war chronicles. Stories about undying loyalty may have been admired because that virtue was so rare in reality.

Yoshitsune's life from 1180 to 1185 (from his arrival in Yoritomo's camp to the beginning of Yoritomo's manhunt) is documented by the *Heike*, Yoritomo's administrative records, and court diaries. However, little is known about his childhood, his teenage years, his fugitive days, or his final hours. Storytellers—the social media of medieval times—enthusiastically filled this vacuum with what we now call fan fiction. Many of these legends involve Benkei, immortalized as a bold and boisterous warrior-monk, and his steadfast friendship during Yoshitsune's darkest days.

People loved Yoshitsune so much that they invented alternative endings to his story. According to some tales, he faked death and escaped north to the island of Hokkaido, where he ruled as king of the barbarians. Others insisted that he jumped on a ship to the Asian mainland, changed his name to Genghis Khan, and conquered China.

The bitter side of Yoshitsune's legacy is seppuku. His uncle Tametomo was the first recorded warrior to kill himself by retiring from the field of battle and cutting his own belly open. Yorimasa, the elderly Minamoto relative who committed seppuku at the Phoenix Hall, near Uji Bridge, was the second. This uniquely brutal form of suicide might have remained an odd historical footnote had Yoshitsune not decided to die in the same fashion— at least according to stories that circulated after Yoshitsune's death. His legend helped turn seppuku into a samurai ideal. Despite what you see in samurai movies, however, seppuku was always an uncommon practice.

In 1689, on the five-hundredth anniversary of Yoshitsune's death, Japan's most famous *haiku* master visited the spot where the great hero died. "Paddies and wild fields have claimed the land where Hidehira's mansion stood," Matsuo Bashō wrote. He recalled the last fight and how "Yoshitsune shut himself up with a chosen band of loyal men—yet their heroic deeds lasted only a moment, and nothing remains but evanescent clumps of grass."

Bashō sat down and wept. Then he wrote this haiku:

A dream of warriors,
and after dreaming is done,
the summer grasses.

More than three hundred years have passed since Bashō inked his poem. Yet Yoshitsune's life and his quest for glory have been remembered and reimagined across the centuries, from medieval songs, *Noh* dramas, *Kabuki* plays, and *Bunraku* puppetry to modern novels, short stories, poems, movies, *manga*, *anime*, visual novels, and video games.

No disrespect, Bashō . . . but Yoshitsune and his dreams live on.

ACKNOWLEDGMENTS

I'm grateful to William Wayne Farris, Sen Sōshitsu Professor of Traditional Japanese Culture and History at the University of Hawai'i, who reviewed my manuscript and provided insightful comments. Many thanks to Karl Friday, Professor Emeritus of Japanese History at the University of Georgia, Japanese sword expert Paul Martin, and Japanese birding expert Kaz Shinoda, who provided answers to questions I couldn't get answered anywhere else.

Yolanda Scott, Editorial Director at Charlesbridge, believed in this project from the start. Senior Editor Alyssa Mito Pusey was exactly the editor every writer wants—smart, supportive, and enthusiastic. Plus she practices a Japanese martial art (aikido)!

Many thanks to Gareth Hinds, who brought Yoshitsune's world to life with his stunning illustrations. And how cool is it that he also practices aikido? I'd also like to thank Art Director Susan Sherman for so adroitly bundling my words and Gareth's art.

I'm grateful to my kid-lit friends Kathy Shepler, Jenni Holm, Deborah Underwood, Keely Parrack, Carol Peterson, Nancy Humphrey Case, and Lesley Mandros Bell, who provided critical advice, critique, and support. My traveling buddies, Dana Kokubun and David Hudson, gracefully endured speed-walking around Kyoto and Kamakura in ungodly heat while listening to me talk for hours about long-dead samurai. My family (husband Rob and children Travis, Kelsey, and Connor) have been unfailingly supportive, even when this entire endeavor appeared quite quixotic.

It has been my great pleasure to practice with my fellow kenshi at the Berkeley Kendo Dojo and the Oakland Kendo Dojo. I owe a special debt to the sensei who have patiently instructed me over the years: Yoshinari Miyata, Sylvette Orlianges, Jason Kim, Will Speagle, Atsushi Miyamoto, Court Tanouye, and especially Bob Matsueda. *Dōmo arigatō gozaimasu.*

AUTHOR'S NOTES

A Note on Names

All names of historical persons in *Samurai Rising* are written using the Japanese convention of family name followed by given name, as in Minamoto Yoshitsune.

Because Japan imported its writing system from China, the Chinese characters (*kanji*) used to write Japanese often have alternative pronunciations: the Chinese reading and the Japanese reading. The kanji used to write "Taira" (the Japanese reading) can also be pronounced as "Heike" (the Chinese reading). For "Minamoto" the Chinese reading is "Genji." The family names of the Taira and Minamoto are always read using the Japanese pronunciation, as in "Taira Kiyomori." However, historians often restrict the use of "Taira" and "Minamoto" to individuals and use the terms "Heike" and "Genji" in a broader sense to include all their retainers and allies. To avoid confusion I have consistently used the terms "Taira" and "Minamoto" throughout this book for both the families of the Taira and Minamoto leaders *and* their followers.

Historians refer to the conflicts of 1180 to 1185 as the Gempei War. "Gempei" combines the kanji character "Gen" from "Genji" and "Hei" from "Heike"; "Genhei" is then softened to the easier-to-pronounce "Gempei."

A Note on Dates

People in twelfth-century Japan used a lunar calendar based on the Chinese model. Each lunar month was about six weeks behind the solar calendar we use today. Every so often the Japanese court proclaimed a new era, and years within that era were numbered. For example, the battle at Ichi-no-Tani occurred on the seventh day of the second month of the third year of the Juei era. In modern times the practice of naming eras has changed; now each era corresponds to an imperial reign. The current Japanese era is called Heisei.

Throughout this book I have retained the Japanese lunar dates for days and months to correspond with the dating found in primary source materials. Years are presented in Western format.

A Note on the Status of Women

The elite women of Heian-period Japan were central to its cultural life. In the eleventh century a woman named Murasaki Shikibu wrote *The Tale of Genji*, the story of an imperial prince named Genji. Many scholars consider Murasaki's work Japan's greatest literary achievement as well as the world's first novel. Sei Shōnagon's witty *Pillow Book* provides another window into this long-lost world of moon-viewing parties, incense-smelling contests, and love affairs conducted mostly through poems and sometimes through secretive shuffles in the night.

Despite the literary prominence of many Heian-era women, we often aren't completely sure of their given names. In those artistic times it was considered classier to refer to an elite woman by a poetic handle, such as "the lady of the willow branches." This ultra-polite tradition may be one reason why highborn women are often referred to only as "the wife [or daughter] of so-and-so."

Samurai women lived in an extremely masculine culture. However, women born into warrior households during Yoshitsune's time could inherit property and serve as landlords, and they also exerted influence behind the scenes. Yoritomo's wife, Hōjō Masako, was involved in power politics for forty-five years. She advised Yoritomo and after his death conspired to rule the country alongside her father and brother. Because she had taken religious vows after Yoritomo's death, she was known as the "nun shogun."

We know very little about the lives of the majority of twelfth-century Japanese women—the peasants, the merchants, the craftspeople. Writing novels, poetry, and diaries was an upper-class hobby. Women in peasant, merchant, and craft families worked alongside their husbands, and their labor was crucial to family survival.

One group of women in early medieval Japan did enjoy a remarkably independent lifestyle. Entertainers like Shizuka came from middle- or lower-class families, but their artistry allowed them to travel freely and mix with all segments of Japanese society. If Shizuka hadn't fallen for Yoshitsune, she would probably have led a full and satisfying life. She was financially independent and could've married—or not—as she chose. Upon retirement she might have opened her own dance academy and filled her later years with the satisfaction of shaping the next generation of artists.

But Shizuka *did* fall in love with Yoshitsune. She *did* publicly defy the lord of Kamakura. I think her courage surpassed that of any other person in this book, Yoshitsune included.

Please note that Shizuka was not a samurai.

Re-creating Yoshitsune's World

It is not easy to reach more than eight hundred years into the past—and into a different culture—to write the story of a person's life. Which sources are the most reliable? How much did the tale change between the happening and the telling? Can the bare bones of fact be used to flesh out the character of a person who died long ago?

As noted earlier, one of my two major sources is *The Tale of the Heike*, as translated by Helen McCullough and Royall Tyler. Historian Paul Varley calls the *Heike* "the finest of the war tales; indeed, it is among the supreme masterpieces of Japanese prose literature."

The other major source is the *Azuma kagami* (*Mirror of Eastern Japan*), a semi-official history of the early years of the Kamakura shogunate. Historians believe it was compiled in the latter half of the thirteenth century from court diaries, family records, temple documents, and early versions of the *Heike*. It is considered the most valuable single source on the origins of Yoritomo's warrior government. I have used Minoru Shinoda's translation, which covers the period 1180 to 1185, and have relied on Hiroaki Sato for translations of later entries mentioning Yoshitsune.

It is difficult to know how much events depicted in *The Tale of the Heike*, the *Azuma kagami*, and other sources were altered or exaggerated to fit the dramatic needs or political agendas of their authors. As scholar and translator Marisa Chalitpatanangune writes, "Although the main events and personages of the [war chronicles] are historical, short fictional elaborations and anecdotes are often incorporated into an account, revealing traces of an oral storytelling tradition."

So how can we know if any individual description or anecdote in the source material is accurate? The short answer is we can't. To be confident of the accuracy of an account, a historian wants multiple records of the event, all recorded shortly after the event by unbiased eyewitnesses. Unfortunately, few historical events eight hundred years in the past can meet this gold standard. We don't know what sort of eyewitness testimony was available to the compilers of the *Heike* and the *Azuma kagami*. And in any case, we must remember that these long-dead authors were writing according to the standards of their own time and culture, not those of twenty-first-century historians. We are forced to make our own judgments about which descriptions and anecdotes are most likely true and which might be invention or elaboration.

Yet there are ways of separating the more probable from the less probable. Historians have noted that some of the information we have about Yoshitsune (for example, his physical description as small, google-eyed, and bucktoothed) runs counter to what we would expect for a heroic figure, even though he is clearly one of the *Heike*'s heroes. The same can be said for some of the most intriguing anecdotes about him: asking his men for advice, losing his bow at Yashima, jumping to another boat at Dan-no-Ura. If the *Heike* described Yoshitsune as a giant among men, broad-shouldered and handsome, a warrior who killed hundreds in a single battle (and so on), we could reasonably dismiss such descriptions as gross exaggerations.

It's much harder to dismiss descriptions and anecdotes that run counter to the heroic ideal. These sorts of things are less likely to be invented.

I have used dialogue from the *Heike*, the *Azuma kagami*, and other sources sparingly. In some cases I have included dialogue because it is the obvious thing someone would say in a situation, and in other cases because the dialogue highlights personality traits that are supported by that person's known actions. Sometimes, however, I have included dialogue in a scene for its historical interest. For example, the *Azuma kagami* notes the death of Kiyomori's nephew Atsumori at Ichi-no-Tani, but the *Heike* gives us a very detailed description of his final moments. Can we be certain that he died exactly the way the *Heike* claims? Can we be certain that before his death Atsumori and his killer had the conversation described in the *Heike*? No and no: we can never be certain. But what the *Heike* shows us, without a doubt, is how Atsumori has been remembered. And that is also a part of Japanese history.

I have provided extensive documentation of my source material and the choices I made in telling Yoshitsune's story. Please see the chapter notes for more detail.

In addition to *The Tale of the Heike*, the *Azuma kagami*, and other sources from Japan's early medieval period, I have drawn from the works of historians, scholars, and translators who specialize in this period in Japanese history. William Wayne Farris, Sen Sōshitsu Professor of Traditional Japanese Culture and History at the University of Hawai'i, kindly reviewed this manuscript prior to publication and I am very grateful for his invaluable expertise and advice.

Of course, nothing can quite compare with visiting the places where events actually took place. Although I lived in Japan for six years during the 1990s and had already visited some of the spots associated with Yoshitsune, I made a special trip to Japan in September 2012. I climbed the steep steps of Kurama Temple, watched horseback archery at Yoritomo's shrine in Kamakura, drank tea alongside the Uji Bridge, hiked the steep hills of Ichi-no-Tani, walked the beaches of Yashima, and dangled my feet in the cold waters of Dan-no-Ura. In Kyoto I strolled down the avenue where Yoshitsune lived, and in Hiraizumi I stood on the ridge where he died.

Only a few structures in Japan have survived the centuries that separate us from Yoshitsune. He might still recognize the beautiful Phoenix Hall beside the Uji River and the radiant Hall of Gold of Hiraizumi. Time, fire, earthquakes, and war have swept away virtually everything else.

Oddly, the bodies of the last rulers of Hiraizumi survived. The mummified remains of Hidehira and Hidehira's father were placed beneath the altar of the Hall of Gold, and a mummified head was stowed in a wooden box next to Hidehira's body. Modern researchers have identified the head as belonging to Yasuhira, the foster brother who betrayed Yoshitsune. The round black lacquer box that held Yasuhira's remains is on display in the museum next to the Hall of Gold. It probably closely resembles the tub that held Yoshitsune's head.

What does linger in places like Kurama, Dan-no-Ura, and Hiraizumi is something timeless: the smallness one feels under a great cedar tree, a cold sea breeze biting the cheek, wind rushing through trees. I hope I have been able to communicate within this book a small measure of what Yoshitsune himself experienced.

That is the "how" of creating this book; the "why" is

more convoluted. While living in Japan I first read *The Tale of the Heike* and fell in love with the story the way I had fallen in love with the tales of King Arthur when I was a teen. Learning that Yoshitsune was a prominent historical figure impressed me all the more.

More than a decade later I found myself looking for a fun way to spend time with my son Connor. I suggested that we try *kendo* (Japanese swordsmanship). Kendo led me back to Yoshitsune and *The Tale of the Heike*. I hope I have done some justice to the memory of Japan's most famous samurai and to the great heritage of Japan's martial arts.

Some argue that over the centuries Yoshitsune's story has been cut and buffed and polished, like a fine diamond, to make it appear brighter, more sparkling, more satisfying than it was in reality. I think the opposite is true. What remains after eight hundred years is only the ghost of Yoshitsune. His reality was surely more intriguing, nuanced, and heartbreaking than anything we can imagine or re-create. What we have, in this or any other form, is nothing more than the fossilized remains of an impossibly complex human experience.

TIME LINES

Yoshitsune and the Wider World

This story takes place in Japan during the last half of the twelfth century. Here's what's going on elsewhere in the world during that time:

Europe is emerging from the Dark Ages; Richard the Lionheart is king of England.

Saladin, the sultan of Egypt and Syria, is successfully defending Jerusalem from European Crusaders who traveled a very long way to pick a fight.

In Mongolia a man named Genghis Khan is getting ready to consume China.

Cambodians are worshipping at a new temple named Angkor Wat.

In West Africa the kingdom of Ghana is falling as the kingdom of Ife rises.

In southern Africa a city now known as Great Zimbabwe is being built stone by stone.

Out in the vast Pacific, the world's greatest seafarers, the Polynesians, have discovered Tahiti. New Zealand, the last major landmass to be settled by humans, is about to lose its Garden of Eden innocence.

In Mexico the Toltec state is collapsing.

High in the Andes the first of the Inca kings is born.

In the Caribbean the peaceful Taino people are blissfully unaware that Columbus will be arriving in about three hundred years.

Major Periods of Japanese History

Paleolithic period: 35,000 BCE to 10,000 BCE. First human occupation of Japan.

Jomon period: 10,000 BCE to 900 BCE. Settlements appear; pottery is invented.

Yayoi period: 900 BCE to 250 CE. Permanent villages, bronze tools, and cloth weaving appear.

Yamato period: 250 to 710 CE. Ancient Japan is ruled by regional chieftains. Buddhism and writing (Chinese script) are introduced. A distinct warrior group (samurai) begins to form.

Nara period: 710 to 794 CE. A centralized state based on Chinese models forms.

Heian period: 794 to 1185 CE. Classical Japan reaches cultural heights; power is centralized in the imperial court.

Kamakura period: 1185 to 1333 CE. Rule by the Kamakura shogunate, established by Minamoto Yoritomo.

Muromachi period: 1333 to 1568 CE. Medieval Japan ruled by the Ashikaga shogunate, but regional lords retain significant power.

Momoyama period: 1568 to 1600 CE. A second flowering of culture; a series of samurai warlords attempt to centralize power.

Edo period: 1600 to 1868 CE. The Tokugawa shogunate rules Japan and largely shuts itself off from the outside world.

Meiji period: 1868 to 1912 CE. Isolation ends as Japan rapidly modernizes. In 1873 Emperor Meiji ends the samurai's exclusive right to be Japan's military force.

Modern period: 1912 CE to present.

Time Line of Samurai Rising

1156: Hōgen Disturbance. Yoshitsune's father allies with Go-Shirakawa, who wins an imperial succession dispute; Yoshitsune's uncle Tametomo allies with the losing side and is banished.

1159: Yoshitsune is born.

1160: Heiji Rebellion. Yoshitsune's father and several of Yoshitsune's older half brothers are killed; his half brother Yoritomo is taken prisoner.

1167: Taira Kiyomori is made chancellor.

1171: Taira Kiyomori's daughter marries the reigning emperor.

1174: Yoshitsune flees north to Hiraizumi.

1178: A son (Antoku) is born to Taira Kiyomori's daughter and the reigning emperor.

1179: Taira Kiyomori imprisons Retired Emperor Go-Shirakawa.

1180, second month: Taira Kiyomori's infant grandson Antoku is named emperor.

1180, fourth month: Prince Mochihito's rebellion is crushed; his ally Minamoto Yorimasa commits suicide.

1180, eighth month: Minamoto Yoritomo, Yoshitsune's half brother, revolts.

1180, tenth month: Battle of Fuji River. Yoshitsune joins Yoritomo.

1180–1182: Drought causes widespread famine. Yoritomo consolidates his position in eastern Japan.

Early 1183: Lord Kiso wins a series of battles against the Taira.

1183, seventh month: The Taira leave Kyoto; Lord Kiso seizes the capital.

1184, first month: Battle of Uji River. Lord Kiso is killed.

1184, second month: Battle of Ichi-no-Tani.

1184, eighth month: Yoshitsune accepts a court title.

1185, second month: Battle of Yashima.

1185, third month: Battle of Dan-no-Ura.

1185, fifth month: Yoshitsune is prevented from entering Kamakura.

1185, tenth month: Attack on Yoshitsune's Kyoto residence.

1185, eleventh month: Yoshitsune disappears.

1186, fourth month: Shizuka dances in Kamakura.

1187, fourth or fifth month: Yoshitsune reappears in Hiraizumi.

1189, fourth month: Assault on Yoshitsune's Koromo River residence.

1189, seventh month: Invasion of Hiraizumi.

GLOSSARY OF JAPANESE WORDS

go (goh): a board game invented in ancient China that is still very popular

haiku (hye-koo): a traditional form of Japanese poetry expressed in three lines with a five-seven-five syllable pattern

kanji (kahn-jee): the Chinese characters used to write Japanese

katana (kah-tah-nah): the classic samurai blade

kumade (koo-mah-day): a pole with an iron claw at the end, used for dragging mounted samurai off their horses

mono no aware (moh-noh noh ah-wah-ray): the poignant awareness of fleeting beauty

naginata (nah-gee-nah-tah): a spear with a curved blade at the end

sake (sah-kay): rice wine

samurai (sah-moo-rye): an armed servant of the nobility

seppuku (seh-poo-koo): ritual suicide

shirabyōshi (shee-rah-byoh-shee): a female artist who danced, sang, and beat a drum

shogun (shoh-goon): originally a military "chief of staff" for the nobility but later the samurai ruler of Japan

tachi (tah-chee): long, curved samurai blade

yamabushi (yah-mah-boo-shee): wandering holy men

CHAPTER NOTES

Here you'll find a compilation of quotation sources, historical details, clarifications, and bits that I think are fascinating but couldn't fit into the main narrative. If you want to know why nobody in the story drinks tea . . . or learn about Go-Shirakawa's obsession with "pop" music . . . or find out what Yoshitsune has in common with Luke Skywalker . . . or discover why Yoritomo didn't use ninjas . . . read on.

For bibliographic information about the sources mentioned in these notes, please see pages 225-231.

1 • DISASTER IN KYOTO

Page 1: Yoshitsune's father: His name was Minamoto Yoshitomo. I have avoided using it because of the confusion of having so many similar names in this book (Yoshitsune, Yoritomo, and Yorimasa, not to mention Kiso Yoshinaka!).

    As the leader of the Minamoto family, Yoshitomo was either incompetent or extremely unlucky, depending on your point of view. In 1156, three years before the battle described in chapter 1, there was a dispute (called the Hōgen Disturbance) within the imperial family over who should be the next emperor. These disputes didn't normally come to blows, but Go-Shirakawa convinced both Minamoto Yoshitomo and Taira Kiyomori to support him over a rival prince. Unfortunately, Yoshitomo's father and brothers sided with the other candidate. After a brief battle Go-Shirakawa's faction emerged victorious. In the aftermath of the Hōgen Disturbance, Yoshitomo was forced to oversee the executions of his father and most of his brothers. His brother Tametomo, the famous archer, was sentenced to banishment and maiming.

(Yoshitomo himself supposedly crippled his brother's shoulders.) By involving samurai in an imperial dispute, Go-Shirakawa revealed the weakness of the imperial family and the true strength of the samurai. The conflict was immortalized in the *Hōgen monogatari* (*Tale of the Hōgen*), compiled in the early thirteenth century. See Wilson, *Hōgen monogatari*, and Tyler, *Before "Heike" and After*, for modern translations.

Page 1: "When one goes . . . as one's horse": Chalitpatanangune, p. 61.

Pages 1–2: The common people of Kyoto: Ruch, pp. 513–14.

Page 2: The political power of Retired Emperors: Farris, *Japan to 1600*, pp. 85–86. "Retired Emperor" is capitalized because it was a formal title, *In*. The institution was known as *Insei*. See Hurst, "Insei."

Page 3: The burning of the palace: Chalitpatanangune, pp. 62–63.

Page 3: "If they sought . . . was saved": Ibid. An alternative translation can be found in Reischauer and Yamagiwa, p. 302.

Page 3: Kiyomori's arms and armor: Chalitpatanangune, p. 117; the *Gukanshō* gives a similar account (Brown and Ishida, p. 115). Warrior tales of this period often provide lovingly detailed descriptions of the horse, armor, and weaponry of the main characters, a tradition that scholars call "dressing the hero" (Varley, *Warriors of Japan*, pp. 63–64). It seems to resemble the way modern-day reporters breathlessly relate the fashions worn by stars on Oscar night. Of course, it is entirely possible that the specific descriptions found in works like *Heiji monogatari* were invented by storytellers. Even if nobody really remembered the exact hue of Kiyomori's or Yoshitsune's armor lacings, however, we know from surviving scroll paintings that these descriptions accurately reflect the general appearance of high-ranking warriors during the early medieval age.

Page 3: The color of Kiyomori's horse: High-ranking samurai seemed to prefer black mounts. At one time or another, the war chronicles mention Yoshitsune's father (Yoshitomo), Kiyomori, Yoshitsune, and Yoritomo riding black warhorses.

Page 4: The number of Kiyomori's warriors: Mass, *Yoritomo*, p. 25.

Page 4: The defeat of the Minamoto forces: Tyler, *Before "Heike" and After*, pp. 129–36.

Page 4: The Retired Emperor's escape: Chalitpatanangune, p. 80.

Page 5: The death of Yoshitsune's father: Ibid., pp. 138–39.

Page 5: Displaying the head of Yoshitsune's father: Brown and Ishida, p. 116. Hanging a head beside the prison gate implied that the dead man was no better than a common criminal (Friday, "Lordship Interdicted," p. 347).

Page 5: The fate of Yoshitsune's older half brothers: Chalitpatanangune, pp. 138, 143–44, 145.

Pages 5–6: Tokiwa's flight: Ibid., pp. 146–54.

Page 6: Tokiwa's meeting with Kiyomori: There are several different versions of this story based on different versions of *The Tale of the Heiji*. In Helen McCullough's translation (*Yoshitsune*, pp. 70–71), Kiyomori "courts" Tokiwa with letters. I have used Tyler's translation (*Before "Heike" and After*, pp. 170–72).

Page 6: Tokiwa's beauty: The story of Tokiwa's selection from a thousand beauties is from Helen McCullough, *Yoshitsune*, pp. 70–71.

Page 6: "Every mother . . . without them": Tyler, *Before "Heike" and After*, p. 171.

A note on ages: Yoshitsune was born in 1159, but we don't know the exact date of his birth. In medieval Japan a person's age was counted according to the number of years he or she had lived in, rather than on a 365-day cycle, so at the beginning of 1160, Yoshitsune's age would have been counted as two, even if he had been born at the end of 1159 and was only a few months old. This is why the given ages of historical figures like Yoshitsune may vary slightly from source to source.

2 • HEADLESS GHOSTS

Pages 9–10: Kyoto during the Heian period: The city's population was probably somewhere between seventy thousand to one hundred thousand people, making it one of the largest cities in the world at the time (William Hoyt McCullough, p. 122).

The Japanese capital was laid out in imitation of the capital of Tang China (Tyler, *Tale of the Heike*, p. xxxv).

Scholars believe that the total population of Japan at this time was somewhere between six million (Farris, *Japan to 1600*, p. 113) and seven million (Souyri, *World Turned Upside Down*, p. 9).

Page 10: History of Kurama: Miller, pp. 216–55.

Page 10: Yoshitsune's early years: Helen McCullough, *Yoshitsune*, p. 13. Although McCullough believes that Yoshitsune arrived in Kurama around age seven, the *Azuma kagami* (Shinoda, p. 190) suggests that he was sent to Kurama while still a baby.

Page 10: Monastic life in Heian Japan: Morris, *Shining Prince*, pp. 89–122; on interiors and lack of heating, ibid., pp. 32–33. If anyone is wondering at the absence of *tatami* mats, what we think of today as tatami (thick mats made of rice straw that often cover an entire floor) were not used during Heian times. Even elites used only thin straw mats (ibid., p. 31).

Page 10: The religious cosmology of early medieval Japan: Breen and Teeuwen, pp. 38–39, 45, 78–79; Bodiford, pp. 167, 172; Ellwood, pp. 100–103; and Kitagawa, pp. 75–80. It should be noted that temples in Japan no longer mix Shintoism and Buddhism as they did in the past. In 1868 the Japanese government decided to "purify" Shintoism and required religious establishments to choose to identify as either Shinto or Buddhist; see Breen and Teeuwen, p. 65.

If you are wondering why this book doesn't mention Zen (the Buddhist sect closely associated with the samurai), it's because Dōgen, the man who introduced Zen into Japan, wasn't born until 1200. Dōgen was the illegitimate son of a Minamoto but was from a different branch of the family than Yoshitsune.

Pages 10–11: Japanese writing: Conlan, pp. 19–49.

Page 11: Reincarnation: Morris, *Shining Prince*, p. 116.

Page 11: Ghosts: Blomberg, *Heart of the Warrior*, p. 116, and Ellwood, p. 103.

Page 11: Illness ascribed to spirits: Murasaki, pp. 165–67.

Page 11: Monkeys: The pink-faced monkey mentioned is the

Japanese macaque (*Macaca fuscata*), which was once widely distributed in forests throughout Japan. These monkeys are the only nonhuman primate species in Japan, and no other nonhuman primate in the world lives so far north. A habituated group of macaques can be visited at Arashiyama Monkey Park near Kyoto.

Page 11: Short-winged hawks: The hawk described is the northern goshawk (*Accipiter gentilis fujiyamae*). Goshawks were the favorite bird of Japanese falconers (Jameson, pp. 5, 9–10). The ferocity of these forest hawks when in pursuit of prey is legendary.

Page 11: Legends about Yoshitsune's boyhood: Yoshitsune's fame originally rested on *The Tale of the Heike*, which focuses on the main Taira-Minamoto conflicts during 1180–1185. Later storytellers couldn't resist filling the void of information about his boyhood and fugitive years. These legends were collected in the 1400s and published in English in 1966 as *Yoshitsune: A Fifteenth-Century Japanese Chronicle*, translated by Helen McCullough. As McCullough notes, the historical value of *Yoshitsune* is limited. According to these stories, supernatural mountain spirits (*tengu*) taught Yoshitsune the art of swordsmanship (think Merlin and young King Arthur, or Obi-Wan Kenobi and Luke Skywalker). The one incident from *Yoshitsune* that I have included in this chapter is the story about Yoshitsune sneaking out to slash trees that he pretended were Taira (Helen McCullough, *Yoshitsune*, p. 75). I think it would be remarkable if Yoshitsune did *not* do something like this, given his family history, his later laser-like focus on becoming a warrior, and the fact that he grew up in a sword culture.

Page 12: Relations between the imperial court and provincial samurai: Friday, "They Were Soldiers Once," pp. 21–52; Friday, "Dawn of the Samurai," pp. 178–88; Helen McCullough, *Genji and Heike*, pp. 245–47; Mass, "Kamakura Bakufu," pp. 46–53; Souyri, *World Turned Upside Down*, pp. 20–22; and Wilson, "Way of the Bow and Arrow," pp. 184–87. As historian Jeffrey Mass has written, "So ingrained was the psychology of a hierarchy in which the center dominated the periphery that in the absence of some regionally based patronage such as the bakufu [the administration later created by Yoritomo], courtiers in the capital, no matter how effete, could remain the superiors of warriors, no matter how powerful the latter were" (Mass, "Kamakura Bakufu," pp. 48–49).

Page 12: The land system: Most land in Japan was either public land, administered by provincial governors on behalf of the emperor, or tax-exempt private land belonging to members of the Kyoto-based aristocracy or the great temples and administered by provincial lords. See Mass, *Warrior Government*, pp. 3–6; Farris, *Japan to 1600*, pp. 84–85; and Segal, "The *Shoen* System," pp. 167–77.

Page 13: "like the two wings of a bird": This is a period description from the *Hōgen monogatari*, as translated by Tyler (*Before "Heike" and After*, p. 44).

Page 13: Kiyomori appointed as chancellor, and the growing power of the Taira: Shinoda, pp. 46–47.

Page 14: "a small, pale . . . bulging eyes": Helen McCullough, *Yoshitsune*, p. 5. This quote is translated from a very early version of the *Heike*; since Yoshitsune is generally treated favorably in the war tales, this unflattering description is probably accurate (Morris, *Nobility of Failure*, p. 74). This description also lends credence to the "dropped bow" incident in chapter 9—as a small man Yoshitsune probably didn't use a very impressive bow.

Page 14: Yoshitsune's brothers: Of Yoshitsune's two full brothers, the middle brother (Gien) left his monastery and joined a local group of Minamoto when Yoritomo's uprising began. He was killed in battle in 1181. The oldest brother (Zenjō) outlived his other siblings and half siblings but was executed for conspiracy at the beginning of the thirteenth century (Helen McCullough, *Yoshitsune*, p. 12).

Page 14: Yoshitsune's escape with the gold merchant: Ibid., p. 13.

Kurama today: Kurama is twelve kilometers (about eight miles) north of Kyoto. All the buildings at Kurama have been burned and rebuilt over the centuries, and none of the present buildings date to Yoshitsune's time. On the way to the main building of the temple complex, the stair-step trail takes you past two massive cedar trees marked with white ropes to indicate their divinity. Given their size and the longevity of cedars, it is possible that Yoshitsune dodged around them when they were saplings. Several specific places at Kurama are associated with Yoshitsune, including a spring he supposedly drank from (possibly true) and a stone he supposedly measured his height against just before running off to Hiraizumi (only if he was the size of a hobbit). Every September Kurama holds a Yoshitsune festival that includes kendo matches fought by young practitioners.

3 • SAMURAI BOOT CAMP

Page 17: Hiraizumi in the late twelfth century: Yiengpruksawan, pp. 1–6, 62, 98.

Page 17: The Hiraizumi Fujiwara (rulers of Hiraizumi): Ibid., pp. 1–5, 62–69, 96–99, 111, 119, 121–26, 161–65, 204, and Mass, *Yoritomo*, p. 134.

Pages 17–18: Minamoto–Hiraizumi Fujiwara relations: When a succession dispute broke out between Hidehira's grandfather Kiyohira and Kiyohira's half brother Iehira over who should rule Hiraizumi, Yoshitsune's great-grandfather Yoshiie rode to battle with Kiyohira (Varley, *Warriors of Japan*, p. 41). See also Yiengpruksawan, p. 58.

Page 18: Roads and barrier stations: Blomberg, *Heart of the Warrior*, p. 101; Von Verschuer, pp. 306–7; and Farris, *Japan to 1600*, pp. 39–40.

Page 18: Agrarian cycles: Farris, *Japan's Medieval Population*, pp. 68–71; Von Verschuer, p. 312; and Adolphson, p. 312.

Page 18: Lives of medieval peasants: Nagahara, p. 326; Souyri, *World Turned Upside Down*, pp. 84–88; Farris, *Japan's Medieval Population*, p. 92; Farris, "Famine, Climate, and Farming," p. 286; and Farris, *Japan to 1600*, pp. 47–48. According to Farris, "Those who survived infancy could expect to live to about age forty" (Farris, *Japan to 1600*, p. 34).

Page 18: Homes of medieval samurai: Hurst, *Armed Martial Arts*, pp. 19–20, and Farris, *Japan to 1600*, p. 100.

Page 18: Conflicts between rural samurai and among families: Souyri, *World Turned Upside Down*, pp. 4–5; Morris, *Shining Prince*, p. 219; and Friday "Lordship Interdicted," p. 48.

Page 19: Entertainers and wayside inns: Goodwin, pp. 27–31, 35, and Souyri, *World Turned Upside Down*, pp. 13–14, 97.

Page 19: Heian-era stories: Examples of the kinds of stories in circulation during Yoshitsune's time can be found in the *Konjaku monogatari* in two different English translations (Ury and Jones).

Page 19: "None of his arrows . . . known to all": This quote, translated from the eleventh-century work *Mutsu waki*, appears in Sato, p. 97.

Pages 19–20: Tametomo: Yoshitsune's uncle seems to have had lifelong behavioral issues. According to the *Hōgen monogatari*, "From childhood no one could stand against him; he would not give way even for his older brothers. Since he behaved utterly without consideration for others, his father, thinking, 'If I keep him with me in the capital something bad is bound to happen,' disowned him and sent him at the age of thirteen down to . . . Kyushu" (Wilson, *Hōgen monogatari*, p. 25).

Pages 19–20: Tametomo's prowess with a bow: Ibid., pp. 37, 39, and Tyler, *Before "Heike" and After*, pp. 44–48.

Page 20: "Let there be . . . them all down": Wilson, *Hōgen monogatari*, p. 25

Page 20: The reason for Tametomo's banishment: Tametomo fought on the losing side in the Hōgen Disturbance of 1156, along with his father and all of his brothers except Yoshitomo, who was the eldest brother and Yoshitsune's father. See the Wilson and Tyler translations of the *Hōgen monogatari*, as well as Blomberg, p. 72.

Page 20: Tametomo's capture and exile: Wilson, *Hōgen monogatari*, pp. 100–107, and Tyler, *Before "Heike" and After*, pp. 95–96.

Page 20: "You men . . . just watch!": Tyler, *Before "Heike" and After*, p. 96.

Pages 20–21: Ritual suicide, or seppuku: The word *seppuku* is the Chinese reading of characters representing "abdomen" and "cut." Medieval Japanese believed that the soul resided in the belly: "The truth of my being is located in the abdomen, therefore I open my abdomen, leaving you to tell whether I am a true being or the simulacrum of a man" (Pinguet, p. 87). See also Fuse, p. 58, and Blomberg, *Heart of the Warrior*, pp. 72–73. Another reading of *seppuku* is *hara-kiri*, a word perhaps better known in the West. See Seward, pp. 13–14.

Page 22: Religious art: One of the blue and gold religious scrolls commissioned by Hidehira can be viewed at the Metropolitan Museum of Art in New York.

Page 22: The training of young samurai: Blomberg, *Heart of the Warrior*, pp. 67–68, 97. I have heard that the most difficult feat in professional sports is hitting a fastball because of the coordination required. I suspect that among all the military arts, horseback archery is probably the most difficult because of the high level of coordination it demands.

Page 22: Samurai tactical coordination: Friday, *First Samurai*, pp. 68–69.

Pages 22–23: Arms and armor: Varley, *Warriors of Japan*, pp. 74–76; Irvine, p. 29; Hurst, *Armed Martial Arts*, pp. 103–31; Sollier and Gyorbiro, p. 27; Friday, *First Samurai*, pp. 69–74; Friday "Valorous Butchers," pp. 2–7; Friday, *Samurai, Warfare*, pp. 68–73, 90–96; and Robinson, pp. 173–90. Although I have mentioned the most common explanation for the placement of the handgrip on the Japanese bow, historian Karl Friday notes that there are other possible explanations (Friday, *First Samurai*, p. 71). Twelfth-century Japanese sleeve armor is called *Yoshitsune-gote* in honor of Yoshitsune (Robinson, p. 185).

Page 23: Japanese horses: Farris, *Japan to 1600*, pp. 81; Friday, *Samurai, Warfare*, pp. 96–99; and Helen McCullough, *Tale of the Heike*, p. 284

Pages 24–25: The Japanese sword: Irvine, pp. 20–29; Friday, *Samurai, Warfare*, pp. 77–85; Farris, *Japan to 1600*, pp. 82–83; and

Hurst, *Armed Martial Arts*, pp. 27–37. As military historian John Keegan notes, "First-quality samurai swords were the best edged weapons that have ever been made" (Keegan, *History of Warfare*, p. 45).

Page 24: Practice with wooden swords: See Hurst, *Armed Martial Arts*, p. 20, and Hurst, "Insei," p. 83. Practitioners of modern martial arts may wonder about *shinai*, the bamboo practice swords now used in kendo. Shinai were not invented until the sixteenth century (Sakai and Bennett, pp. 129–31, 155). The protective equipment now used in kendo dates from the mid-1800s (ibid., p. 187).

Page 25: Shining for deer: Friday, "Dawn of the Samurai," pp. 183, 188.

Page 25: Kiyomori's spies: Tyler, *Tale of the Heike*, pp. 12–13.

Page 25: The marriage of Kiyomori's daughter and the birth of Antoku: Brown and Ishida, p. 122, and Mass, *Yoritomo*, pp. 22–23, 29.

Pages 25–26: Kiyomori's relations with the Kyoto elite: Mass, *Yoritomo*, pp. 29–33.

Page 26: Kiyomori's moves against Go-Shirakawa: Takeuchi, p. 697; Hurst, "Insei," p. 629; and Mass, *Yoritomo*, pp. 20–21.

Page 26: The rebel prince and Minamoto Yorimasa: Prince Mochihito was the second son of Retired Emperor Go-Shirakawa. See Shinoda, pp. 48–49, and Takeuchi, pp. 697–98, for more on their rebellion.

Page 26: "In recent years . . . your house": Tyler, *Tale of the Heike*, pp. 283–84.

Page 26: Yorimasa during the Heiji Rebellion: Ibid., p. 241.

Page 27: Yorimasa's reputation as a poet: Ibid., p. 242.

Page 27: "their corpses . . . great stream": Helen McCullough, *Tale of the Heike*, p. 237.

Page 27: The Phoenix Hall: Now the main temple of the Byōdō-in Monastery, this sublime building—arguably the most beautiful in all Asia—is still standing near the Uji Bridge. It was originally part of a residence for a high-ranking Kyoto aristocrat. The temple was dedicated in 1052, and the hall was completed in 1053 (Tyler, *Tale of the Heike*, p. 226, footnote).

Page 27: "This forgotten tree . . . turns to sorrow": Ibid., p. 235.

Page 27: Yorimasa's suicide: Helen McCullough, *Tale of the Heike*, pp. 156–57. The *Azuma kagami* tells the story differently. It says that Yorimasa was killed by the Taira and his head "pilloried," while the rebel prince killed himself—though the method of suicide is not described (Shinoda, p. 153). It should be noted that Tametomo and Yorimasa (if the *Heike* version is correct) were not the first warriors to commit suicide. Others sometimes fell on their swords rather than be killed by enemies. Seppuku, as introduced by Tametomo and Yorimasa (or at least these two were the first recorded practitioners), involved both removing oneself from the immediate field of battle and dying from a self-inflicted cut to the abdomen. Many other bits were added (Yorimasa seems to have added the writing of a death poem) over the centuries until seppuku became a kind of performance art (Seward, pp. 41–71).

Page 28: Yoritomo's in-laws: Souyri, *World Turned Upside Down*, p. 49, and Shinoda, pp. 57–59.

Page 28: Yoritomo in exile: Oyler, p. 32.

Page 28: Yoritomo's precarious situation in 1180: Friday, "They Were Soldiers Once," pp. 39–42; Mass, *Yoritomo*, pp. 67–69; and Mass, "Kamakura Bakufu," p. 138.

Page 29: Yoshitsune's departure from Hiraizumi: Shinoda, p. 190. As translated by Minoru Shinoda, the *Azuma kagami* says that Yoshitsune "stole out of Hidehira's manor." Later, Hidehira, "forgetting his selfishness," orders two samurai brothers to join Yoshitsune. This tidbit implies that Yoshitsune was living in Hidehira's household and that Hidehira had grown close to his foster son.

The involvement of great temples: Several large Buddhist temples, along with their warrior monks, supported Prince Mochihito's rebellion against Taira Kiyomori. Afterward, in retaliation, Kiyomori ordered the temples burned to the ground. This deeply offended Kyoto society and helped turn the populace against the Taira (Takeuchi, pp. 703–4). Although the great temples comprised the third force in early medieval Japanese politics, along with the Kyoto aristocracy and the samurai, for simplicity's sake I have not gone into detail about their involvement in the events surrounding the Gempei War.

4 • BROTHERS-IN-ARMS

Pages 31–32: Yoritomo's "new deal": Segal, *Coins, Trade*, pp. 122–23, 143; Takeuchi, pp. 702–3; Mass, "Kamakura Bakufu," pp. 52–53; Mass, *Yoritomo*, pp. 69–76; Farris, *Japan to 1600*, pp. 108–9; and Souyri, *World Turned Upside Down*, p. 40.

Page 32: Cordial relations between the Minamoto and their Taira overlords: Shinoda, p. 57.

Page 32: Tax and rent payments: For a discussion of commodities used for tax and rent payment, see Segal, *Coins, Trade*, p. 3, and Von Verschuer, pp. 312–19.

Pages 32–33: Yoritomo's men attack the Taira official: Shinoda, pp. 161–63.

Page 33: Yoritomo's narrow escape in the Ishibashi Mountains: Ibid., pp.165–68.

Page 33: The Kannon in Yoritomo's hair: Ibid., p. 168.

Page 33: "There are no traces . . . mountain": Ibid.

Pages 33–34: Yoritomo's success in gathering troops: Ibid., pp. 60–63.

Pages 33–34: The Minamoto connection to Kamakura: Collcutt, pp. 90–119, and Mass, *Yoritomo*, p. 77.

Page 34: Yoritomo's pardoning of the man who shot at him: Shinoda, pp. 196–97.

Page 34: Tadanobu and Tsuginobu: Hidehira's choice of Tadanobu and Tsuginobu, "known for their bravery," is mentioned in the *Azuma kagami* (Sato, p. 153). It should be noted that there is some discrepancy in references to who was the elder brother (Tyler, *Tale of the Heike*, p. xlvi versus p. 593). Also, Shinoda's translation from the Japanese is "Tsugunobu" (Shinoda, p. 190). However, I have used "Tsuginobu" in keeping with both Tyler's and Helen McCullough's *Heike* translations.

Page 35: Teeth blackening: Teeth were blackened using a varnish made from iron filings mixed with sake, tea, or urine. It may have originated as a way of hiding teeth blackened by decay—making a virtue of poor dental care. The phrase "wild and barbaric," in reference to non-blackened teeth, is from a well-known Heian-era story about a woman who refuses to submit to social pressure to conform to the current standards of beauty. Blomberg, "Strange White Smile," pp. 243–51. For a full translation of "The Lady Who Admired Vermin" (I loved the lady as soon as I read that title), see Helen McCullough, *Classical Japanese Prose*, pp. 256–63.

Page 35: "Once a rider . . . keeps on fighting": Helen McCullough, *Tale of the Heike*, p. 188.

Pages 35–36: Drought and famine in 1180: Farris, *Japan's Medieval Population*, p. 30.

Page 36: The battle of Fuji River: Shinoda, pp. 188–89, and Helen McCullough, *Tale of the Heike*, p. 190.

Page 36: Waterfowl: I could not resist trying to figure out exactly what sort of water birds would be resting on the Fuji River at dusk eight hundred autumns ago. According to Japanese birding guide Kaz Shinoda, the only waterfowl resident all year long in that area is the eastern spot-billed duck (*Anas zonorhyncha*). However, the birds aren't terribly gregarious. Another candidate is the black-tailed gull (*Larus crassirostris*). The most intriguing possibility is a big flock of migrating geese—either greater white-fronted geese (*Anser albifrons*) or bean geese (*Anser fabalis*). Although large flocks of these migratory geese are not found along the Fuji River today (the area is quite a bit more developed than it was in Yoshitsune's time), tens of thousands still gather in the fall in central Hokkaido, the northernmost of the large Japanese islands. If a vast flock did congregate on the Fuji River in fall 1180 and then launch into the air at nightfall, it would've indeed been impressive and intimidating (Kaz Shinoda, personal communication, 2013).

Page 36: "The great [Minamoto] . . . surrounded!" and "leaped . . . picket stakes": Helen McCullough, *Tale of the Heike*, p. 190.

Pages 36–37: Yoshitsune's arrival at Yoritomo's camp: Shinoda, pp. 189–90.

Page 37: Regional differences in armor: See chapter 7 note on recognizing others during a battle (pages 202–3).

Page 37: The differences between eastern and western accents: Souyri, *World Turned Upside Down*, p. 13.

Page 37: "the two . . . wept with joy": Shinoda, p. 190.

Page 38: "Build no halls . . . I require": Helen McCullough, *Tale of the Heike*, p. 211.

Page 38: Kiyomori's death: Ibid., pp. 209–11.

Page 39: The famine of 1180–1182: Farris, *Heavenly Warriors*, pp. 305–6, and Farris, *Japan's Medieval Population*, pp. 30–33.

Page 39: Peasant survival strategies during famines: Farris, *Japan to 1600*, p. 67.

Page 39: Disease: Ibid., pp. 114–16.

Page 39: "Countless people . . . to pass": Helen McCullough, *Classical Japanese Prose*, pp. 384–85.

Page 39: Yoritomo's consolidation of the east: Shinoda, pp. 72–80.

Page 39: "had been a secluded . . . stand in a line": Ibid., p. 77.

Page 39: Samurai pastimes at Kamakura: Ibid., pp. 78–79, 232, 236. I wish I could tell you more about "ox chasing" (*ushi-oumono*), but I haven't been able to find any details.

Page 40: Noriyori and the status of the Minamoto half brothers: Helen McCullough notes that Noriyori's mother was a harlot who worked at a post station (Helen McCullough, *Yoshitsune*, p. 12, footnote). If a man had multiple wives or concubines, the relative status of the sons was based on their mother's status rather than birth order. Yoritomo's mother had a higher-status background than Yoshitsune's or Noriyori's, so for that reason, more than primogeniture, he was the acknowledged heir. Yoshitsune's mother, Tokiwa, had been simply a high-end maid, but she ranked higher than a common prostitute. As a result, even though Yoshitsune was younger than Noriyori, his rank within the family hierarchy was somewhat higher.

In Heian Japan, marriages were strictly private affairs— in other words, neither the state nor religious institutions were involved. So the "legitimacy" of children was a fuzzy thing. Generally, if a man recognized a child as his, the child was considered legitimate. We don't know how Noriyori proved his status as Yoshitomo's son, but there is no mention of anyone questioning it. For a discussion of the relative status of wives and concubines, see Morris, *Shining Prince*, pp. 217–24.

Page 40: Yoritomo scolds Yoshitsune: Shinoda, p. 221.

Page 40: "How can you say such a thing?": Ibid.

Page 40: The birth of Yoritomo's son: Ibid., p. 237.

Page 41: Yoshitsune in 1182 and 1183: In the *Azuma kagami*, the semi-official record of the Kamakura shogunate, Yoshitsune isn't mentioned at all during the year 1182. All entries for 1183 are missing from the document, so we don't really know what Yoshitsune was doing during this time, other than cooling his heels in Kamakura. See Shinoda, p. viii.

Page 41: Kiso Yoshinaka: Yoshinaka's full name was Minamoto Yoshinaka, but most scholars refer to him as "Kiso Yoshinaka" or "Lord Kiso" in reference to his home base in Kiso. I have kept that tradition, since it also helps to distinguish him from all the other Minamoto whose names begin with Y.

Page 41: The Taira battles against Lord Kiso: Helen McCullough, *Tale of the Heike*, p. 225, and Shinoda, pp. 81–82.

Page 41: "Now is the time to do just that": This quote comes from the *Gukanshō* (as translated by Brown and Ishida, p. 135), a study of Japanese history written in 1219. The author of the *Gukanshō* is repeating a story he says was told by one of Go-Shirakawa's ministers.

Page 42: The Taira departure from Kyoto: Helen McCullough, *Tale of the Heike*, pp. 243, 245, 255, and Shinoda, p. 82. Rokuhara, the Taira "suburb" east of the capital, is described in Hurst, "Insei," p. 628.

Page 42: Elite homes and furnishings: Helen McCullough, "Aristocratic Culture," pp. 390–95.

Page 42: The sacred mirror, sword, and jewel: Ashkenazi, pp. 80–87.

Page 42: The sun goddess and the imperial line: Breen and Teeuwen, p. 29.

Page 43: Go-Shirakawa's flight to Kurama: Helen McCullough, *Tale of the Heike*, p. 242.

Page 43: Lord Kiso's entrance into Kyoto: Ibid., p. 257.

Page 43: Go-Shirakawa's rewards to Lord Kiso: Shinoda, p. 82.

Page 43: Lord Kiso's abuses: Helen McCullough, *Tale of the Heike*, p. 275. See Oyler, p. 66, for more on Kiso's background and lack of sophistication.

Page 43: "With all the checkpoints . . . shallow water": Helen McCullough, *Tale of the Heike*, p. 282.

Page 44: The role of the imperial family: William Hoyt McCullough, pp. 123–24.

Page 44: Religious rituals: Breen and Teeuwen, p. 32.

Page 44: Relations between Yoritomo and Go-Shirakawa: Mass, *Yoritomo*, pp. 84–86; Mass, *Warrior Government*, p. 72–73; Souyri, *World Turned Upside Down*, pp. 44–45; and Shinoda, pp. 83 and 113.

Page 44: Yoritomo gives command to Yoshitsune and Noriyori: Shinoda, pp. 84–85.

Kamakura today: The shrine complex that honors Hachiman, patron god of the Minamoto, still overlooks Kamakura. The structures do not date from Yoritomo's time because the shrine has burned and been rebuilt over the years. However, many places in Kamakura still echo Yoritomo's rule. Wakamiya Ōji (Young Prince Avenue), built by Yoritomo in honor of his son Yoriie's birth, remains Kamakura's main street. The Drum Bridge at the entrance to the shrine is a duplicate of the bridge Yoritomo first built in 1182. The joined ponds in front of the shrine are known as the Gempei Ponds (Minamoto-Taira Ponds). It is said that Yoritomo's wife, Masako, insisted that the Minamoto Pond should have three islands but that the Taira should have four. In Japanese one pronunciation of "four" is *shi*, which also means death.

Since 1187 the Hachiman shrine has been the site of a

ceremonial *yabusame* (horseback archery) competition which takes place every September along a long track on the temple grounds. The participants and shrine officials dress in costumes of the twelfth and thirteenth centuries.

5 • PERILOUS RIVER

Page 47: The layout and appearance of Kyoto: William Hoyt McCullough, pp. 106–7, and Hall, pp. 3–21. Rashōmon provides the title to Akira Kurosawa's famous film.

Page 48: Yoshitsune's armor: Helen McCullough, *Tale of the Heike*, pp. 289–90, and Meech-Pekarik, p. 109.

Page 48: Samurai armor and accessories: Varley, *Warriors of Japan*, pp. 74–76; Irvine, p. 29; Hurst, *Armed Martial Arts*, pp. 103–31; Sollier and Gyorbiro, p. 27; Friday, *First Samurai*, pp. 69–74; Friday, "Valorous Butchers," pp. 2–7; Friday, *Samurai, Warfare*, pp. 68–73, 90–96; and Robinson, pp. 173–90.

Page 48: Failure to wear helmets: Tyler, *Tale of the Heike*, p. 227.

Page 50: Tadanobu and Tsuginobu: Neither is specifically mentioned as being with Yoshitsune at the Uji River. It is highly likely they were there, however, since they are mentioned in subsequent battles as among his closest companions.

Pages 50–51: Size of the armies: According to the *Azuma kagami*, Yoshitsune and Noriyori led "several tens of thousands of troops" (Shinoda, p. 246). Historians think this is a vast exaggeration. Helen McCullough believes Yoshinaka had only about one thousand men, while Yoshitsune had three to four thousand men (Helen McCullough, *Yoshitsune*, pp. 15–16). Another historian thinks Yoshinaka had about six to seven thousand men in total; if a third of these faced Yoshitsune at Uji, and Helen McCullough's estimates of Yoshitsune's forces are correct, then Yoshitsune had less of a numerical advantage (Takeuchi, p. 706).

Page 51: Samurai war bands: Friday, *First Samurai*, pp. 68–69, and Friday, "Valorous Butchers," pp. 13–14. As historian Karl

Friday writes, "Careers were determined by reputations built on individual prowess. Thus officers as well as warriors of lesser stature were, like modern professional athletes, more apt to think of themselves as highly talented individuals playing *for* a team rather than as components *of* a team" (Friday, *First Samurai*, p. 68).

Page 51: "What shall . . . subside?," "It is . . . either," and "I'll test it for you!": Helen McCullough, *Tale of the Heike*, p. 287.

Page 52: First man across the Uji: There is a bit of backstory to the competition over becoming the first man across the Uji River. According to *The Tale of the Heike* (Helen McCullough, pp. 284–88), a samurai named Kagesue asked Yoritomo to allow him to ride the famous horse Ikezuki to war. Instead, Yoritomo gave Kagesue his second-best horse, Surusumi ("Ink Stick"). He gave Ikezuki to another samurai named Takatsuna. Takatsuna promised Yoritomo that astride Ikezuki he would be sure to be the first man across the Uji River. But as Yoshitsune's men jostled for position on the banks of the Uji, Takatsuna feared that Kagesue might get the jump on him. He told Kagesue that his girth looked loose; the momentary distraction allowed Takatsuna to surge ahead. Kagesue and his horse Surusumi eventually reached the opposite bank but landed far downstream.

Page 52: The battle of Uji River: Helen McCullough, *Tale of the Heike*, pp. 287–88.

Page 53: Kiso Yoshinaka's military defense of Kyoto: Shinoda, pp. 85–86, and Helen McCullough, *Tale of the Heike*, p. 284.

Page 53: Lord Kiso leaves Kyoto: Helen McCullough, *Tale of the Heike*, pp. 289–90. Those already familiar with *The Tale of the Heike* will notice, and perhaps vehemently object to, my failure to include Tomoe Gozen in my account of Kiso Yoshinaka's last stand. According to the *Heike*, Tomoe was a female warrior, "a remarkably strong archer, and as a swordswoman she was a warrior worth a thousand, ready to confront demon or god, mounted or on foot." The *Heike* claims that Tomoe was one of the last few loyal retainers to protect Lord Kiso, and only left him when he told her it would dishonor him to have kept a woman with him during his last battle. After taking one last enemy head, Tomoe discarded her armor and fled east (ibid., pp. 291–92). Unfortunately, as historian Paul Varley notes, "Although scholars have valiantly sought to identify Tomoe as a historical figure, they have thus far been unable to adduce evidence sufficient to prove that she is other than a creation of the *Heike*'s authors" (Varley, *Warriors of Japan*, p. 104).

Page 54: Horseback archery tactics: Friday, *First Samurai*, pp. 73–74, and Friday, *Samurai, Warfare*, pp. 104–34.

Page 54: Lord Kiso's death: Helen McCullough, *Tale of the Heike*, p. 293. It is worth noting that the *Gukanshō* (Brown and Ishida, p. 140) claims that Yoshitsune pursued Lord Kiso into a rice field, where he was beheaded by Yoshitsune's friend Ise Saburō. However, both the *Heike* and the *Azuma kagami* say that Kiso was killed by Noriyori's men. I think the most likely scenario is that Yoritomo told Yoshitsune and Noriyori that whoever got to Kyoto first should secure Retired Emperor Go-Shirakawa before worrying about finishing off Lord Kiso. This would account for the story of Yoshitsune's immediate ride to the capital to find Go-Shirakawa as related in the *Heike*, and seems more consistent with Yoritomo's way of operating—he always kept his eyes on the prize.

Page 54: Lord Kiso's head hung next to the prison gate: Shinoda, p. 247.

Page 54: Yoshitsune rides to the Retired Emperor: Helen McCullough, *Tale of the Heike*, p. 289.

Page 54: "arrived . . . open the gate!": Tyler, *Tale of the Heike*, p. 461.

Page 55: Date of leaving Kyoto for Ichi-no-Tani: Yoshitsune entered Kyoto on the twentieth day of the first month of 1184 and left for the Taira lines on the twenty-ninth day of the first month (Shinoda, pp. 246–47).

Page 55: Samurai kidnapping peasants: Farris, *Japan to 1600*, p. 130.

Uji today: Uji is now a quiet little suburb of Kyoto that smells faintly of the green tea for which it is famous. Today the Uji River flows calmly between concrete banks, and the modern bridge carries four lanes of Toyotas and Nissans. The Phoenix Hall (part of the Byōdō-in), where Minamoto Yorimasa committed suicide, is the only building that remains from Yoshitsune's time. The owners of the Tsuen tea shop on the opposite side of the river claim descent from a samurai who fought on the Minamoto side during the Heiji Rebellion of 1160; the tea shop itself is more than three hundred years old. The nearby Tale of Genji Museum provides insight into the graceful Heian culture that warriors like Yoshitsune brought to an end.

6 • MIDNIGHT STRIKE

Page 57: The fortifications at Ichi-no-Tani and Ikuta-no-Mori: Helen McCullough, *Tale of the Heike*, pp. 295–96.

Page 58: Taira strategy at Ichi-no-Tani and Ikuta-no-Mori: Friday, *Samurai, Warfare*, pp. 122–23, 130.

Page 58: Size of the armies: Historian Helen McCullough estimates that the size of the defending force at Ichi-no-Tani was twenty thousand men, and writes that it is unlikely that the Minamoto had many more warriors than were available for their recent fight with Lord Kiso (estimated at six to eight thousand men, counting both Yoshitsune's and Noriyori's forces—see note on page 195) and that the number may have been as low as two to three thousand men (Helen McCullough, *Yoshitsune*, pp. 16–17).

Pages 58–61: Departure from Kyoto and path of Minamoto armies: Shinoda, pp. 248–49.

Page 58: Yoshitsune's horse: Helen McCullough, *Tale of the Heike*, p. 366.

Page 60: Yoshitsune's meeting with Go-Shirakawa: Ibid., p. 298.

Page 60: The expense of equipping a samurai: Farris, *Japan to 1600*, p. 81.

Pages 60–61: Benkei the warrior-monk: In Japan, Benkei's fame rivals Yoshitsune's. According to legend, after leaving Kurama the teenage Yoshitsune didn't go straight to Hiraizumi. Instead, he spent some time lurking around Kyoto, disguised as a temple page. As Yoshitsune was walking across the Gojo Bridge in Kyoto, he ran into Benkei. The boisterous warrior-monk had vowed to collect one thousand swords in order to pay for the rebuilding of a temple that he had accidentally burned down. Yoshitsune was a small, slim teen and seemed an easy mark. However, Yoshitsune defeated Benkei in a David-and-Goliath-type duel and afterward insisted that the warrior-monk become his follower. See Helen McCullough, *Yoshitsune*, pp. 109–31, for a translation of these beloved and very entertaining stories. Benkei's fame rests mostly on these legends; he is mentioned only briefly in *The Tale of the Heike* and the semi-official history *Azuma kagami*. His first appearance in both sources is at Ichi-no-Tani.

Pages 60–61: Warrior-monks: According to historian Mikael Adolphson, warrior-monks were not monks who became warriors, but warriors who became monks and used their skills within a monastic context (Adolphson, pp. 87–121).

Pages 60–61: Yoshitsune's companions: In addition to Benkei, *The Tale of the Heike* lists Ise Saburō, Tsuginobu, and Tadanobu as being among Yoshitsune's forces during the Ichi-no-Tani campaign (Helen McCullough, *Tale of the Heike*, p. 301). This inner circle would later include Washinoo, a hunter's son. As historian Paul Varley notes, "No other commander in the *Heike* has such an odd and socially inferior assortment of followers" (Varley, *Warriors of Japan*, p. 134).

Pages 61–62: The night attack: Shinoda, p. 249, and Helen McCullough, *Tale of the Heike*, pp. 301–2. As historian Karl Friday notes, "Early medieval Japanese concepts of honor and of honorable conduct in battle appear to have been flexible enough to permit successful warriors to rationalize almost any behavior" (Friday, "What a Difference," pp. 57–58). See also Friday, *First Samurai*, p. 44; Friday, "Might Makes Right," pp. 168–69; and Friday, "What a Difference," pp. 64, 76–77, for discussions of the samurai sense of "fair play."

Page 62: Samurai treatment of noncombatants: Friday, *Samurai, Warfare*, pp. 158–59.

Page 62: "in light as bright as day" and "the ones . . . and quivers": Helen McCullough, *Tale of the Heike*, p. 302.

Pages 62–63: Noriyori's arrival at Ikuta-no-Mori: Ibid., p. 303.

Page 63: Yoshitsune splits his forces: Ibid.

Pages 63–64: The search for the Hiyodorigoe Cliffs: Ibid., pp. 303–5.

Page 64: "Excellent advice": Ibid., p. 303.

Page 64: "Why, it sounds . . . deer goes": Ibid., p. 305.

Page 64: Definition of "samurai": In later centuries "samurai" would become a rigid class with entry strictly regulated by birth. However, during the twelfth century, samurai were "servants and officers of the powers-that-were, not a ruling order unto themselves"; they were "defined more by craft than by pedigree, and drawn from the lower and middle ranks of the court nobility and the upper tiers of rural society" (Friday, *Samurai, Warfare*, p. 156). At least until Yoritomo, with Yoshitsune's help, transformed the samurai's place in Japanese society.

Page 65: Flute music from Ichi-no-Tani: Helen McCullough, *Tale of the Heike*, p. 317.

Pages 65–66: "The full-drawn bows . . . spring breeze": Ibid., p. 295.

Page 66: "Keep pushing . . . the face": Ibid., p. 307.

Page 66: "Their shouts . . . falling rain": Ibid., pp. 310–11.

Page 67: Yoshitsune's band: Ibid., p. 311. According to the *Heike*, Yoshitsune had thirty men with him; according to the *Azuma kagami* (Shinoda, p. 249), he had seventy men. Thirty seems more likely given that it was a stealth attack.

Page 67: "All right . . . I do!": Helen McCullough, *Tale of the Heike*, p. 311.

7 • HOOVES LIKE HAILSTONES

Page 69: "The fierce combat . . . penetration": Shinoda, pp. 249–50.

Pages 69–70: The battle of Ichi-no-Tani: Ibid., and Helen McCullough, *Tale of the Heike*, pp. 310–12. Description of the battlefield: Helen McCullough, *Tale of the Heike*, p. 319.

Page 69: "Ei! Ei!": Ibid., p. 311.

Page 70: Yoshitsune after the ride down the cliffs: You may be wondering what Yoshitsune did during the battle after forcing open the gates at Ichi-no-Tani. The answer is that we don't know. He was probably riding around with his companions picking off Taira.

Page 70: Battlefield chaos: Friday, "Valorous Butchers," p. 18.

Page 70: Foot soldiers' weapons: Ibid., pp. 4–5.

Page 71: Swords on horseback: Despite what you sometimes see in Japanese movies about Yoshitsune, samurai of this period didn't use bladed weapons from horseback (Friday, *Samurai, Warfare*, p. 131). There is one exception, however: the commander at Ichi-no-Tani had his arm cut off by a Minamoto riding up from behind (Helen McCullough, *Tale of the Heike*, p. 314). Presumably the swordsman was out of arrows.

Page 71: Bamboo grass reddened with blood: Helen McCullough, *Tale of the Heike*, p. 319.

Page 71: The death of Kiyomori's brother: Tadanori was the commander-in-chief of the Taira forces at Ichi-no-Tani, and, for the record, fought better than most. Ibid., pp. 313–14.

Pages 71–72: The horse that followed his master: The warhorse's name was Inoueguro, or "Inoue Black," because he was bred at Inoue in Shinano, which was part of Lord Kiso's home territory. The horse had once been a favorite of Retired Emperor Go-Shirakawa's. In those days high-ranking nobles and samurai often exchanged gifts of horses, and some years before, the Retired Emperor had given him to Kiyomori's son Munemori, who then gave him to his brother Tomomori, the commander-in-chief at Ikuta-no-Mori. At least the horse's story has a happy ending: after the battle at Ichi-no-Tani, he was returned to Go-Shirakawa. Ibid., pp. 318–19.

Page 72: "He will fall . . . kill him" and "It makes no . . . Don't shoot": Ibid., p. 318.

Page 72: "men of quality" and "and they ended . . . Ichi-no-Tani": Ibid., p. 312.

Pages 72–74: The Taira youth: The death of Atsumori, the teenager who is killed by the Minamoto warrior Kumagae Naozane on the beach, is one of the most famous stories in the entire *Tale of the Heike* (Helen McCullough, pp. 315–17). Historian Paul Varley writes: "The *Heike* is full of brave—sometimes insanely brave—acts by warriors in battle. But few elicit our admiration as does Atsumori's, largely because it is truly a *beau geste*, a noble but meaningless gesture, as though a courtier had symbolically sacrificed himself to a fierce warrior as the warrior was about to overrun his world" (Varley, *Warriors of Japan*, p. 111).

Page 72: "It is dishonorable . . . Return!": Helen McCullough, *Tale of the Heike*, p. 316.

Page 73: "I am a desirable . . . my head": Ibid., p. 317.

Page 73: Kagetoki's personality: The *Gukanshō* says, "He was painfully self-centered and was contemptuous of those under him" (Brown and Ishida, p. 179).

Page 74: The taking of heads: Since one side in the battles of this age usually had the cover of an imperial mandate, those on the opposite side were automatically criminals. This was probably a factor in the harsh treatment of those on the losing side (Friday, "What a Difference," pp. 68–71). The description of the exposure of the Taira heads is from Shinoda, p. 251.

Page 74: Medicine on the battlefield: Goble, pp. 311–12, 315. A fourteenth-century Japanese medical manual helpfully suggests this method for determining the depth of a wound: "use an arrow and you will know" (Goble, p. 315).

Recognizing opponents on the battlefield: I did wonder how the Minamoto and Taira could tell each other apart on the battlefield during the disorganized melee that must have occurred, since they didn't fight in ranks. Did they wear armbands? According to historian Karl Friday: "Basically, there was no over-arching scheme by which warriors in early medieval Japanese battle could recognize enemy troops other than by location (did they seem to be defending the place you were attacking or vice versa?) or by recognizing individuals or members of particular families by the colors and lacings of their armors. . . . There was definitely no use of armbands, tunics, or other common colors or symbols worn by all troops in a unit or side—although commanders at various levels did make use of banners, and there may be some historical reality to the idea—described in literary texts like the *Heike monogatari*—of Yoritomo's side using white banners, while Kiyomori and his allies used red ones" (Karl Friday, personal communication, 2011). The colors of the Japanese flag and the strips of cloth worn by practitioners of kendo during matches are inspired by the Taira and Minamoto colors—an echo of those long-dead combatants. See Smith, p. 170.

In addition, notable Japanese lineages had family crests (*mon*). The Minamoto crest was a combination of gentian flowers and bamboo leaves, while the Taira crest was a swallowtail butterfly. Although there is no mention in the *Heike* of these crests being used on battle banners, they were certainly used for decorative purposes. We have incorporated both mon into this book's design.

Ichi-no-Tani today: Ichi-no-Tani was located at Suma Beach. (Suma is a suburb of Kobe.) There is a cable car that takes passengers up the Hiyodorigoe Cliffs, and trails climb through the forest to the ridge overlooking the site of Ichi-no-Tani. The *Heike* makes it sound as though Yoshitsune and his men dropped down a vertical cliff, which isn't true, or at least isn't true of the spot today. However, descending Hiyodorigoe remains a challenging scramble for a person on foot and an insane place to ride a horse—much like the famous downhill gallop in the movie *The Man from Snowy River*, but with more foliage to overcome.

8 • INTO THE STORM

Page 77: The construction of a Japanese sword: Irvine, p. 9; Sakai and Bennett, pp. 65–71; and Friday, *Samurai, Warfare*, pp. 84–85.

Page 77: Taira departure to the west: Shinoda, p. 86.

Page 78: The Minamoto's lack of boats in eastern Japan: Ibid., pp. 88–89.

Page 78: Yoritomo's courting of eastern warriors: Ibid., p. 88, and Mass, "Kamakura Bakufu," pp. 57–58. An announcement to "the local lords of the nine provinces of Kyushu" is translated by Shinoda, pp. 254–55.

Page 78: Yoritomo's insistence on the right to reward warriors: Shinoda, pp. 90–92, summarizes the powers Yoritomo requested in a document sent to Go-Shirakawa after the victory at Ichi-no-Tani. The document became one of the foundations for warrior rule in Japan.

Page 78: Expansion of Yoritomo's powers: Mass, "Kamakura Bakufu," pp. 56–57.

Page 78: Yoshitsune's appointment as Yoritomo's deputy: Helen McCullough, *Yoshitsune*, p. 17.

Page 78: Poor sanitation in Kyoto: Farris, *Japan to 1600*, p. 60.

Page 78: Aristocratic homes: Ibid., pp. 72–73.

Pages 78–79: Aristocratic life and culture in Kyoto: Varley, "Cultural Life," pp. 448, 452–53; William Hoyt McCullough, pp. 97–182; and Helen McCullough, "Aristocratic Culture," pp. 390–448. The best insight into the aristocratic culture of Heian Japan is found in Murasaki Shikibu's *The Tale of Genji*, as well as Sei Shōnagon's *Pillow Book* (Helen McCullough, *Classical Japanese Prose*, pp. 156–99). Both of these famous female authors wrote their masterpieces around the year 1000, about 180 years before the main events of *Samurai Rising*.

During Yoshitsune's time even the elite probably needed lots of incense to mask body odors, particularly during Kyoto's murderously hot and humid summers. The Japanese custom of frequent bathing was several hundred years into the future (Farris, *Japan's Medieval Population*, p. 91).

If you are wondering why nobody in the story ever sips tea, it's because tea drinking didn't become established in Japan until the 1200s. During Yoshitsune's time, tea was considered a medicine. Later generations of samurai—ironically inspired by the delicate aesthetics of the aristocratic age they trampled underfoot—would create the Japanese tea ceremony ritual (William Wayne Farris, personal communication, 2014).

Page 79: Aristocratic women using screens for modesty: Morris, *Shining Prince*, p. 211.

Page 79: Women's robes: The colors and patterns of robes are taken from *The Tale of Genji* (Murasaki, pp. 406–7). Although written about 180 years prior to Yoshitsune's time, they do represent Heian-era aristocratic dress.

Page 79: Teeth blackening: See note for chapter 4 on page 191.

Page 79: Shirabyōshi dancers: Ruch, pp. 526–30; Goodwin, pp. 28–29; and Souyri, *World Turned Upside Down*, pp. 96–97. *The Tale of Giō*, a story within the larger *Tale of the Heike*, tells of two shirabyōshi dancers who become Taira Kiyomori's mistresses. The story includes a brief description of shirabyōshi technique. Helen McCullough, *Tale of the Heike*, p. 30. And if you're wondering why there are no geisha in this story, it's because the geisha tradition was not established until the nineteenth century.

Pages 79–80: "lightning flashed . . . three days": Helen McCullough, *Yoshitsune*, p. 226.

Page 80: Yoshitsune and Shizuka's first meeting: Ibid., p. 221. Go-Shirakawa might have had a hand in introducing Yoshitsune to Shizuka. Despite his exalted rank, the Retired Emperor adored the kind of popular songs that Shizuka sang. He was such a fan, in fact, that he invited an elderly songstress named Otomae to live in his palace so he could learn her repertoire. (Imagine Queen Elizabeth asking a rapper to move into Buckingham Palace!) Otomae did become Go-Shirakawa's teacher, and when the old lady fell deathly ill, the Retired Emperor visited Otomae's bedside to sing a song she had taught him that was reputed to have healing power. Otomae was brought to tears by this kindness. Ruch, pp. 528–29, and Kim, pp. 1–22.

Page 80: The timing of military campaigns: Samurai were reluctant to leave their estates until their crops had been harvested, and of course it was important to have a good enough harvest to support a military campaign (Souyri, *World Turned Upside Down*, pp. 35–36). I think fall was a good time for war for another reason: nobody in their right mind would fight in full armor during the stifling Japanese summer.

Page 80: Yoshitsune quells warrior unrest: Mass, *Warrior Government*, p. 78, and Mass, *Yoritomo*, pp. 88–89.

Page 80: Tokiwa's daughter: Arnn, p. 151, and Helen McCullough,

Yoshitsune, p. 13. It is said that after Kiyomori tired of Tokiwa, he married her off to a minor official.

Page 81: Recognition of Noriyori over Yoshitsune: Shinoda, pp. 94–97, 269–70.

Page 81: Financial rewards of governorships: Von Verschuer, pp. 314, 319, and Segal, "The *Shoen* System," p. 173.

Page 81: Yoshitsune's popularity in Kyoto: As historian Helen McCullough notes, Yoshitsune was "well liked by the proud court aristocrats and treated with marked distinction by the ex-Emperor himself" (Helen McCullough, *Yoshitsune*, p. 17). The *Heike* says that Yoshitsune was "at home in the capital" (Helen McCullough, *Tale of the Heike*, p. 357). See also Morris, *Nobility of Failure*, p. 102.

Page 82: Go-Shirakawa's awards to Yoshitsune, and Yoritomo's response: Shinoda, pp. 94–97, 274.

Page 82: Court rankings: Court rankings went in reverse order, from nine to one, with one being the highest. Fifth rank was important, because there was a very big jump in status between ranks nine to six and ranks five and above (William Wayne Farris, personal communication, 2014). Third rank or above was reserved for the true elite, who were the highest councils of government (Helen McCullough, "Aristocratic Culture," pp. 130–33). A junior fifth rank, as Go-Shirakawa gave to Yoshitsune, came with a land grant, which was the equivalent of being awarded a government salary. It was also a special honor (Tyler, *Tale of the Heike*, p. xxxi).

Pages 82–83: Yoshitsune's marriage: We don't know the name of Yoshitsune's wife, only that she was the daughter of a man named Kawagoe Tarō Shigeyori (Shinoda, pp. 276–77). For an explanation of the reluctance to use personal names for women, see pp. 167–68 and Tyler, *Tale of the Heike*, p. xxxviii.

Pages 82–83: Marriage and the status of women: Moeshart, pp. 27–31.

Page 83: The layout at Yashima: Helen McCullough, *Yoshitsune*, p. 19.

Page 83: Noriyori's campaign: Shinoda, pp. 89, 273.

Page 83: Provisioning by samurai armies: Farris, *Japan to 1600*,

p. 118. As historian William Wayne Farris writes, "In the end it usually came down to stealing cultivators' food en route and at the battle scene. . . . No wonder cultivators fled battlegrounds, hid their possessions, and generally detested samurai" (Farris, *Japan's Medieval Population*, p. 63).

Page 83: Armor during a long campaign: Historian Julia Meech-Pekarik quotes a Japanese armorer who says that "on a long and difficult campaign [armor] becomes evil smelling and over-run by ants and lice" (Meech-Pekarik, p. 110).

Pages 83–84: "because of the shortage . . . native provinces": Shinoda, p. 287.

Page 84: Yoshitsune's accomplishments versus Noriyori's: Japanese historian Minoru Shinoda notes that "what Yoshitsune was able to accomplish in the next few weeks—a result Noriyori had failed to achieve in months—constitutes one of the more brilliant chapters in the annals of Japanese military history" (Shinoda, p. 98).

Page 84: "I shall not return . . . China" and "I intend . . . can reach": Helen McCullough, *Tale of the Heike*, p. 358.

Page 84: Yoshitsune leaves Kyoto: Shinoda, pp. 97–98.

Page 84: The size of Yoshitsune's strike force: Helen McCullough, *Yoshitsune*, p. 19 (footnote).

Page 86: Kagetoki's rank: Historian and translator Hiroaki Sato notes that Kagetoki's field rank "was nominally far below that of someone like Yoshitsune, who bore the title of *sō-daishō* (general of the army), but Kagetoki regarded himself as Yoritomo's *o-daikan* (special deputy) and would not easily defer to his direct superior in the field, Yoshitsune" (Sato, p. 116).

Page 86: The reverse-oars controversy: Helen McCullough, *Tale of the Heike*, pp. 358–60.

Page 86: "What are reverse oars?," "the usual equipment," "A good Commander-in-Chief . . . him," and "I don't know . . . and win": Ibid., p. 359.

Page 87: "a little fresh," "Shoot down . . . boats," "Whether . . . stayed behind," and "We must not . . . hold back": Ibid., p. 360.

Page 88: Japanese ships: Farris, *Japan to 1600*, p. 70.

Pages 88–89: The crossing to Shikoku and Victory Beach:

Shinoda, pp. 291, 297, and Helen McCullough, *Tale of the Heike*, pp. 360–61.

Page 89: "How far is it to Yashima from here?" and "Two days": Helen McCullough, *Tale of the Heike*, p. 362.

Pages 90–91: "Who is the . . . today?," "as a gold . . . his back," "Keep . . . my master!," "They tell . . . [banditry]," and "So ended . . . words": Ibid., p. 364.

Pages 90–91: The battle at Yashima: Ibid., pp. 362–66, and Shinoda, pp. 292–93, 297.

Kyoto today: Fire and earthquakes have destroyed almost everything from Yoshitsune's time. However, the temple Sanjusan-gendo was built by Taira Kiyomori in honor of Retired Emperor Go-Shirakawa; although most of it burned down in 1249, some of the original statues were saved, and the building was reconstructed in 1266. Every year an archery competition is held along the outside of the long, narrow hall. You can still walk along Rokujō, the avenue where Yoshitsune's Kyoto residence was located, and at one end of Gojo Bridge there is a cartoonish statue of Yoshitsune and Benkei fighting (it depicts the legend about their first meeting).

9 • THE DROPPED BOW

Page 93: Tsuginobu's death: Helen McCullough, *Tale of the Heike*, pp. 363–66. The *Heike* mentions the gift of Yoshitsune's horse immediately after Tsuginobu's death, probably for dramatic purposes. While this grand gesture is in line with what we know of Yoshitsune's character, it seems highly unlikely that the confrontation on Yashima was halted so that a monk could be summoned. I have placed the horse giving after the fighting was over. As far as we know, Tsuginobu was the first of Yoshitsune's close friends to die.

Pages 94–96: The fan incident: Ibid., pp. 366–68. This scene is quite famous, and as recounted in the *Heike* has a very

courtly quality. But the Taira and the Minamoto weren't guests at a garden party; they were people who wanted each other dead. So did the fan incident actually happen, and did it happen as recorded in the war chronicle? It is true that archery contests were a popular entertainment among the Japanese elite, and given the boredom of the long standoff at Yashima, it's reasonable to believe that a fan was set up as a lure or a taunt. However, I think there might have been a level of nastiness to the scene that doesn't come across in the elegant *Heike*. To wit: the hanging of the fan meant "Try to hit *this*, jerks." The dance was a sarcastic "Oh, look, the jerk hit the fan." Yoshitsune's order to murder the dancer requires no translation.

Page 95: "You men . . . right now": Ibid., p. 367.

Page 95: Arrowheads used by early medieval samurai: Blomberg, *Heart of the Warrior*, pp. 49–50, and Friday, *Samurai, Warfare*, p. 71.

Page 96: Standing shields: Friday, *Samurai, Warfare*, p. 89.

Page 96: "overlapped . . . wings": Helen McCullough, *Tale of the Heike*, p. 369.

Pages 96–97: The dropped bow: Ibid., pp. 368–70. This quirky incident reveals several interesting things about Yoshitsune. First, he wasn't a very big man, since he couldn't draw a very big bow, which supports the physical description we have of him. Second, it hints at Yoshitsune's interest in his dead uncle Tametomo, who he would later imitate in other ways. Third, it suggests a kind of casual intimacy with his brothers-in-arms that helps us understand why he was so popular with the Minamoto troops.

Page 96: "Let it go!": Ibid., p. 370.

Page 97: "I would have . . . Yoshitsune'": Ibid.

Pages 97–98: The Taira council and the last battle on Shikoku: Ibid.

Page 99: Kagetoki's arrival: Ibid., pp. 371–72.

Page 99: "as useless . . . for the rite": Tyler, *Tale of the Heike*, p. 602.

Page 99: Gathering of the Minamoto navy: Shinoda, pp. 298–99.

Page 99: "The eastern warriors . . . climb trees": Helen McCullough, *Tale of the Heike*, p. 374.

Yoshitsune's leadership: It is interesting to note the parallels between the leadership styles and tactical genius of Yoshitsune and Alexander the Great. Although far removed from each other in time and culture, they both led from the front and typically found a chink in the spot where their enemies felt most secure; once this spot was breached, the enemy was usually completely demoralized and broke ranks. "Total exposure to risk was his secret of total victory," John Keegan writes of Alexander. This was Yoshitsune's secret as well. For a discussion of Alexander's tactics, see Keegan, *Mask of Command*, pp. 13–91.

Yashima today: Yashima is near the city of Takamatsu on Shikoku Island. The shallows between Yashima and Shikoku have been completely filled in, so Yashima is no longer an island. The view from Yashima Temple (on the flat-topped mountain) is lovely, and a "blood pond" near the temple is supposed to be the site where the Minamoto washed their swords after their victory. There is also a tradition of lobbing clay disks off the mountaintop to symbolize the Minamoto samurai discarding their helmets after the battle. That scenario is extremely unlikely, to say the least. They all knew they had another battle to fight.

10 • THE DROWNED SWORD

Page 101: Yoshitsune's preparations: Shinoda, p. 98.

Page 101: Rakes used in battle: Friday, *Samurai, Warfare*, pp. 87–88.

Pages 101–2: The navies: Helen McCullough, *Tale of the Heike*, pp. 372–73. Little is known about Japanese ships from this era (Farris, "Shipbuilding").

Pages 101–9: The battle of Dan-no-Ura: Shinoda, pp. 98–99, 299–301, and Helen McCullough, *Tale of the Heike*, pp. 372–80.

Page 102: The number of combatants at Dan-no-Ura: Helen McCullough, *Yoshitsune*, p. 20 (footnote).

Page 102: Kagetoki's ancestor: Helen McCullough, *Tale of the Heike*, p. 310.

Pages 102–3: Yoshitsune's conflict with Kagetoki: Ibid., p. 373.

Page 102: "I might . . . myself": Ibid.

Page 103: "This lord . . . men!" and "You are . . . Japan!": Tyler, *Tale of the Heike*, p. 604.

Page 105: "fair-skinned . . . buck teeth": Helen McCullough, *Tale of the Heike*, p. 374.

Page 105: "a fighter" and "He's too small . . . throw him in": Tyler, *Tale of the Heike*, p. 606.

Page 105: "Our side is winning!": Helen McCullough, *Tale of the Heike*, p. 375.

Page 107: "Yesterday's subordinates . . . masters": Ibid., p. 376.

Page 107: "You will be . . . warriors": Ibid., p. 377.

Page 107: "Where . . . Grandmother?" and "This land . . . awaits us": Tyler, *Tale of the Heike*, p. 610.

Page 107: The drowning of Antoku: Ibid., pp. 609–11, and Helen McCullough, *Tale of the Heike*, pp. 376–78.

Page 108: The sacred jewel: There is some discrepancy about the fate of the jewel (which is also sometimes described as a string of beads). According to one passage in the *Heike*, Kiyomori's widow takes it with her when she drowns herself and Emperor Antoku (Tyler, *Tale of the Heike*, p. 610). But elsewhere, the *Heike* says the jewel was retrieved from a box found floating at Dan-no-Ura (ibid., p. 620). The sword lost at Dan-no-Ura was presumably replaced with a copy. The regalia still exist, though what the objects actually look like remains a mystery. No photos or drawings are allowed, and the regalia may be viewed only by the emperor and certain Shinto priests.

Page 108: The deaths and attempted drownings of high-ranking Taira: Helen McCullough, *Tale of the Heike*, pp. 378–79.

Page 109: "suspecting anyone finely equipped": Tyler, *Tale of the Heike*, p. 615.

Page 109: Noritsune at Dan-no-Ura: Ibid., and Helen McCullough, *Tale of the Heike*, pp. 378–80.

Dan-no-Ura today: The straits of Dan-no-Ura lie off the modern-day city of Shimonoseki. A monument along the

211

shore depicts Yoshitsune's leap to another boat to avoid being killed by Noritsune.

11 • ASSASSINS IN THE DARK

Page 111: Yoshitsune's leap to another boat: Yoshitsune's previous actions demonstrate an obvious cool under fire, so his avoidance of Noritsune can best be interpreted as wiliness rather than fear or panic. The *Heike* mentions that during the battle Yoshitsune switched his armor in an attempt to keep from being targeted by Taira samurai (Helen McCullough, *Tale of the Heike*, p. 374). By escaping from Noritsune rather than confronting him, Yoshitsune was denying the Taira even the possibility of revenge. Unheroic, maybe—but smart.

Page 112: "Fine, you're coming with me": Tyler, *Tale of the Heike*, p. 617.

Page 112: The death of Noritsune: Ibid., pp. 616–17, and Helen McCullough, *Tale of the Heike*, pp. 379–80.

Page 112: The aftermath of battle: Helen McCullough, *Tale of the Heike*, p. 381.

Page 112: Messages about victory: Shinoda, p. 302.

Page 112: Go-Shirakawa's congratulations to Yoshitsune and Yoritomo: Ibid., pp. 302, 304.

Pages 112–13: Yoritomo's orders to Noriyori and Yoshitsune: Ibid., pp. 303–4, 310.

Page 113: "make every effort to retrieve the Sacred Sword": Ibid., p. 310.

Page 113: Women divers: Brown and Ishida, p. 143.

Page 113: Beliefs about the sacred sword: Ibid., pp. 143–44, and Helen McCullough, *Tale of the Heike*, p. 386.

Page 113: "most adept with words": Shinoda, p. 142.

Pages 114–17: Yoritomo's rift with Yoshitsune: Mass, *Yoritomo*, p. 99.

Page 114: "Although Yoshitsune . . . attendance on Yoshitsune": Shinoda, pp. 305–6.

Pages 114–15: The return of the sacred jewel and mirror to Kyoto:

Ibid., p. 306, and Helen McCullough, *Tale of the Heike*, pp. 383, 388.

Page 115: Yoshitsune's clothing reported to Yoritomo: Shinoda, p. 123.

Page 115: Noriyori's complaints: Ibid., p. 311.

Pages 115–16: Viewing of the Taira captives: Ibid., p. 307, and Helen McCullough, *Tale of the Heike*, pp. 386–88.

Page 116: Yoshitsune's letter to Yoritomo: Shinoda, p. 311.

Page 116: The order for Yoritomo's vassals to stop serving Yoshitsune: Ibid., p. 308.

Page 116: "had abused . . . subservience to him": Ibid.

Page 117: Yoshitsune's second marriage: Tyler, *Tale of the Heike*, p. 631. It is unclear whether Yoshitsune was obligated to seek Yoritomo's permission to wed, but it would've been politically wise to do so, especially since the woman was a Taira and the daughter of a captive. It is worth noting that in 1179 Yoritomo also married into the family that was holding him prisoner.

Page 117: "a little old": Ibid.

Page 117: The Iris Festival: For the Heian court calendar, see Morris, *Shining Prince*, pp. 156–65.

Page 117: Everyday life in Kyoto: Ruch, pp. 512–14.

Pages 118–19: Yoshitsune in Koshigoe: Shinoda, pp. 313–20, and Helen McCullough, *Tale of the Heike*, pp. 392–94. According to some sources, Yoshitsune and Yoritomo did meet briefly, though Yoshitsune was not allowed to discuss matters with Yoritomo and was brusquely sent away (Oyler, pp. 97–98). However, both the *Azuma kagami* and *The Tale of the Heike* describe Yoshitsune waiting fruitlessly in Koshigoe for a meeting that is never allowed.

Pages 118–19: "Minamoto Yoshitsune . . . committed no wrong": Shinoda, pp. 316–17. The full text of the letter appears in much the same form in both the *Azuma kagami* (ibid.) and the *Heike* (Helen McCullough, *Tale of the Heike*, pp. 393–94, and Tyler, *Tale of the Heike*, pp. 637–38). However, historians are unsure if this is a copy of a real letter or if it was something created by early *Heike* authors as a dramatic way of portraying Yoshitsune's state of mind and his precarious situation, and then copied by the compilers of the *Azuma kagami*. (Manpukuji Temple in Koshigoe claims to display the original letter—supposedly dictated by Yoshitsune and written by Benkei—but historians dismiss it as a later forgery.) It is certainly possible that Yoshitsune fashioned a written appeal to his brother if he realized he would not be allowed to plead his case in person. If this letter is historically accurate, it reveals a very proud and stubborn man who is incapable of humbling himself even when his life depends on it. See Oyler, pp. 86–114, for a detailed analysis.

Page 119: "Action is expected later": Shinoda, p. 316.

Page 119: The execution of Taira Munemori: Ibid., pp. 323–24; Helen McCullough, *Tale of the Heike*, pp. 396–97; and Brown and Ishida, p. 145. Yoritomo ruthlessly hunted down and killed every other Taira male not captured or killed at Dan-no-Ura. It is said that during the first year after their victory, Yoritomo's men did "everything but open the mothers' wombs in their zeal to hunt down and kill even those [Taira] sons who were a mere year or two old" (Helen McCullough, *Tale of the Heike*, p. 422).

Page 119: Yoritomo confiscates Yoshitsune's lands: Shinoda, p. 321.

Page 120: Yoshitsune's inaction: Morris, *Nobility of Failure*, p. 87.

Page 120: Six nasty things before breakfast: To be fair, Yoritomo could be magnanimous, such as when he forgave many of the men who fought against him and almost killed him in the mountains (chapter 4). He did not, however, extend such grace to members of his own family, whom he persecuted with astonishing zeal.

Page 120: The earthquake: Helen McCullough, *Tale of the Heike*, p. 401, and Brown and Ishida, p. 146.

Pages 120–21: Kagetoki's son's visit to Yoshitsune in Kyoto: Shinoda, p. 336. It is clear by this point that Yoritomo was already completely convinced of Yoshitsune's disloyalty and was looking for any excuse to make the final move. Yoritomo's messenger was Kajiwara Kagesue (ibid.), the eldest son and heir of Kajiwara Kagetoki (Helen McCullough, *Tale of the Heike*, p. 373).

Page 121: Yoshitsune's illness: Helen McCullough translates the "self-inflicted burns" noted in the *Azuma kagami* account as "moxa cautery," or burns from moxa, a herbal remedy made of dried mugwort (Helen McCullough, *Yoshitsune*, p. 25). Burning moxa against the skin was a Chinese medical practice used to treat beriberi, a disease caused by a lack of vitamin B1 (thiamine) in the diet. Weakness and emaciation are symptoms of this condition. Beriberi was common among the Kyoto elite because of their reliance on polished rice, which is deficient in vitamin B1. In those days there was no such thing as a daily vitamin pill. A description of Heian-era diets can be found in Farris, *Japan's Medieval Population*, p. 92.

Page 121: Yukiie's prior history: Shinoda, pp. 84–85.

Page 122: "There is not . . . [for rebellion]": Ibid., p. 336.

Page 122: The recruitment of Shōshun: Yoritomo's retainers didn't jump at the chance to kill Yoshitsune. According to the *Azuma kagami*, while Shōshun volunteered, "many others had excused themselves"—which for Yoritomo probably indicated silent support for his half brother and counted as yet another reason to eliminate Yoshitsune (ibid., p. 337).

If you are wondering why Yoritomo didn't hire ninjas to kill Yoshitsune, you watch too many cheesy movies. Ninjas didn't exist until several centuries later, and even then were more myth than reality. See Souyri, "Autonomy and War," pp. 110–123, for ninja origins.

Page 122: Shōshun's visit to Yoshitsune: Helen McCullough, *Tale of the Heike*, pp. 405–6, and Tyler, *Tale of the Heike*, pp. 656–57.

Page 122: "Well? . . . Lord Yoritomo?": Tyler, *Tale of the Heike*, p. 657.

Page 123: The attack on Yoshitsune's mansion: Shinoda, p. 339, and Helen McCullough, *Tale of the Heike*, pp. 406–7. In the *Azuma kagami* version, Uncle Yukiie arrives to help

Yoshitsune. However, Yukiie isn't mentioned in the *Heike* account.

The site of Yoshitsune's Kyoto home today: From a reference in the *Azuma kagami*, it appears that the site of Yoshitsune's residence was near the spot where Muromachi-dori crosses Rokujō (Shinoda, p. 339). If you follow Rokujō down to the Kamo River, you'll find the site where the would-be assassin Shōshun was executed.

12 • SHIZUKA'S SONG

Page 125: The attack on Yoshitsune's mansion: See note for chapter 11 on pages 215–16.

Pages 125–26: Shōshun's capture and execution: Helen McCullough, *Tale of the Heike*, pp. 406–7, and Shinoda, p. 344.

Page 126: "This is what . . . all those oaths": Tyler, *Tale of the Heike*, p. 659.

Page 126: Yoshitsune's imperial mandate: Shinoda, p. 339; Helen McCullough, *Tale of the Heike*, p. 407; and Souyri, *World Turned Upside Down*, pp. 45–46.

Pages 126–27: Yoritomo's reaction: Shinoda, pp. 343–44.

Page 127: The failure of other samurai to join Yoshitsune: Morris, *Nobility of Failure*, p. 96.

Page 128: Yoshitsune's failure to pillage Kyoto: The courtier Kanezane—although a Yoritomo partisan—wrote in his diary: "It must be said that Yoshitsune behaved like a gentleman" (Helen McCullough, *Yoshitsune*, p. 26, footnote).

Page 128: Yoshitsune's departure from Kyoto and his fight with Yoritomo partisans: Shinoda, pp. 345–46; Helen McCullough, *Tale of the Heike*, p. 408; and Brown and Ishida, p. 147. The *Azuma kagami* says that Yoshitsune was accompanied by another uncle, the younger brother of his mother, Tokiwa. This implies that during his time in Kyoto, Yoshitsune did re-establish a relationship with his maternal relatives.

Pages 128–29: The storm at sea: Shinoda, p. 346; Helen McCullough, *Tale of the Heike*, p. 408; and Helen McCullough, *Yoshitsune*, p. 156.

Pages 129–32: Shizuka in the Yoshino Mountains: Shinoda, p. 351.

Page 129: "when Yoshitsune . . . courage failed": Helen McCullough, *Yoshitsune*, p. 168. Despite the quote's literary rather than historical nature, I have included it because it probably accurately depicts the fitful and agonizing way Yoshitsune was forced to part from Shizuka. The *Azuma kagami* report reads simply: "There she parted from him" (Shinoda, p. 360).

Page 130: Yoritomo returns to Kamakura: Shinoda, p. 347.

Page 130: "search the mountains . . . early date": Ibid., p. 348.

Page 130: "as there are monks . . . removed": Ibid., p. 357.

Page 130: Yoritomo's punishment of people associated with Yoshitsune: Ibid., pp. 355, 357, 364.

Page 130: "was undoubtedly the work of the devil": Ibid., p. 350.

Page 131: "So long as . . . the one mentioned": Ibid., p. 351.

Page 131: The expansion of Yoritomo's powers: Mass, "Kamakura Bakufu," pp. 59–60; Mass, *Warrior Government*, p. 118; Shinoda, pp. 353–54; Helen McCullough, *Yoshitsune*, p. 27; Souyri, *World Turned Upside Down*, pp. 45–46; and Segal, "The *Shoen* System," p. 175.

Page 131: "seize and use . . . families": Shinoda, p. 354.

Page 132: Shizuka abandoned in the mountains: Helen McCullough, *Yoshitsune*, pp. 169–71.

Page 132: "blood from . . . scarcely move": Ibid., pp. 169–70.

Page 132: "strange and eerie": Shinoda, p. 351.

Page 133: Hachiman shrine: Collcutt, p. 105.

Pages 133–34: Shizuka in Kamakura: Shizuka's appearance before Yoritomo is described in the *Azuma kagami* as translated by Sato (pp. 148–50). A story about the incident composed much later appears in Helen McCullough, *Yoshitsune*, pp. 225–36. See also Collcutt, pp. 105, 111.

Page 133: "the amazed . . . clouds rang": Helen McCullough, *Yoshitsune*, p. 234.

Page 134: "Would that I . . . Yoshino's peaks": Ibid., pp. 234–35.

Hachiman shrine today: A small shrine (Wakamiya) on the grounds of the temple is said to be the spot where Shizuka sang and danced. Her performance is re-created every April during Kamakura's spring festival.

13 • THE FUGITIVE

Page 137: Fear of the mountains: Souyri, *World Turned Upside Down*, p. 14.

Page 137: Yamabushi: Kasahara, pp. 314–31, and Blomberg, *Heart of the Warrior*, pp. 34–35.

Page 138: Straw snow boots: Ury, p. 106.

Page 138: Clothing in medieval Japan: Nagahara, pp. 324–25, and Farris, *Japan's Medieval Population*, p. 91. Cotton was not in common use in Japan until the sixteenth century.

Page 138: Yoshitsune's whereabouts during 1186–1187: Helen McCullough provides a translation and summary of historian Kuroita Katsumi's work on where Yoshitsune and his friends sought sanctuary while in the Kyoto area (Helen McCullough, *Yoshitsune*, pp. 297–301). Most likely they were helped and hidden by sympathetic monks; in those days some of the larger Japanese temples enjoyed a certain amount of independence. Kuroita also believes that Retired Emperor Go-Shirakawa may have helped hide Yoshitsune and his companions, at least until it became too dangerous to do so.

Pages 139–40: The legend about Tadanobu's battle at Yoshino: This story and the quotes drawn from it appear in Helen McCullough, *Yoshitsune*, pp. 175–189.

Page 139: "Let me delay . . . you escape": Ibid., p. 175.

Page 139: "with a good grace," "When you become . . . exhausted man," and "This weapon . . . for mine": Ibid., p. 176

Pages 140–42: The story of the river crossing and the quotes drawn from it: Ibid., pp. 189–96.

Page 141: "It's much easier . . . all of you": Ibid., p. 193.

Page 141: "It was . . . jump across," "Don't pay any attention to him," and "Your legs . . . your tongue": Ibid., p. 194. In the first quotation, "onto" has been corrected to "on to."

Page 141: "Everyone makes mistakes": Ibid., p. 195.

Pages 142–43: The legend about passing the barrier: Ibid., pp. 59–61. This story was first developed as a short Noh drama called *Ataka*. It was later turned into a popular Kabuki play titled *Kanjinchō*. In the hands of Japanese filmmaker Akira Kurosawa, it became the 1945 film *The Men Who Tread on the Tiger's Tail*.

Page 143: "So he looks . . . his life" and "It's been . . . like this?": Ibid., p. 60.

Page 143: The capture of the head monk of Kurama: See the *Azuma kagami* as translated by Sato (pp. 147–48).

Page 143: The capture of Yoshitsune's mother, Tokiwa: The *Azuma kagami* says that early in 1186 Tokiwa and her daughter were seized in Kyoto in an attempt to find out where Yoshitsune was hiding (Arnn, p. 151). We don't know if Tokiwa's daughter was fathered by Taira Kiyomori or by Tokiwa's second husband, a minor official. Tokiwa's fate, and her daughter's, is unknown.

Page 143: The capture of Yoshitsune's servant: Sato, pp. 147–48.

Pages 143–44: Childbirth rituals: Farris, *Japan to 1600*, p. 132.

Page 144: The death of Shizuka's baby: A dramatization of this event can be found in Helen McCullough, *Yoshitsune*, pp. 219–25. These stories imagine that Shizuka gives birth before her dance at the Hachiman shrine. However, as McCullough notes, in the *Azuma kagami* the dance occurs while Shizuka is still pregnant (ibid., p. 56). Since the *Azuma kagami* is the more reliable source, I have followed that chronology. See also Arnn, pp. 161–68. Shizuka and Yoshitsune's newborn son was drowned at Yuigahama, now a popular beach near Kamakura.

Page 144: "Tadanobu, being . . . subdued": Sato, p. 152.

Page 144: The death of Tadanobu: Ibid., pp. 152–53.

Page 144: The rumor of Yoshitsune's suicide: See Helen McCullough's translation of Kuroita Katsumi's work (Helen McCullough, *Yoshitsune*, p. 300).

Page 144: Yoshitsune's path north: Historian Helen McCullough suggests that Yoshitsune and his band traveled to Hiraizumi along the Hokurikudō (a road that followed the northern coastline of Honshu) using their yamabushi disguises (ibid., p. 28).

Literary depictions of Yoshitsune: Many later tales about Yoshitsune on the run portray him as hesitant, passive, and deeply dependent on Benkei. As historian Helen McCullough notes, the medieval Japanese audience was "profoundly influenced by what we may call the Heike fallen-warrior tradition fostered by *Heike monogatari* [The Tale of the Heike]: the concept of a once-mighty warrior hounded by fate, divested of his military attributes, and transformed into an elegant, ineffectual courtier" (ibid., pp. 35–36).

14 • FEAST OF ARROWS

Page 147: Yoshitsune's home in Hiraizumi: Ibid., pp. 275–76.

Page 148: Yoshitsune's wife and child: The *Azuma kagami* reports a rumor that Yoshitsune took a wife, a son, and a daughter with him to Hiraizumi, "all . . . either in the guise of itinerant mountain monk or child" (Sato, p. 153). However, only a four-year-old girl is mentioned in the later *Azuma kagami* entry describing Yoshitsune's suicide (ibid., p. 155). What happened to the son mentioned in the rumor? The following possibilities exist: 1) the first entry in the *Azuma kagami* about a son is wrong, and there was only ever a daughter; 2) there was a son, who died of natural causes before his parents' suicide; 3) the later entry about only a daughter dying with her parents is wrong, and a son died also; or 4) a son somehow survived. The first possibility seems most plausible. It's highly unlikely that a son and heir of Yoshitsune would have been overlooked or allowed to escape. Yoritomo was just too thorough.

Page 148: Games popular among men: Morris, *Shining Prince*, p. 148.

Page 148: Hunting and falconry: Jones, p. 83, and Ury, pp. 121–22, 198.

Page 148: Hunting in Hiraizumi: Yiengpruksawan, pp. 111, 118. Hidehira actually had scenes of himself hunting painted inside a Hiraizumi temple. This was somewhat shocking, since the taking of life is prohibited in Buddhism (though the samurai routinely ignored this prohibition). For more about hunting and Buddhism, see Vollmer, pp. 200–201.

Pages 149–55: Yoshitsune's last battle: Hidehira's death and his last wishes, Yasuhira's attack on Yoshitsune, and Yoshitsune's suicide are recorded in the *Azuma kagami* as translated by Sato, pp. 154–56. A much more elaborate description appears in Helen McCullough, *Yoshitsune*, pp. 285–292. The account in *Yoshitsune* follows the broad strokes of the account in the *Azuma kagami*. Although it is dramatized, I have relied on it as the best approximation of Yoshitsune's end, with one exception. As noted above, the *Azuma kagami* says that one child of Yoshitsune's (a daughter) died alongside Yoshitsune and his wife. The dramatized account in *Yoshitsune* claims that two children died: a five-year-old boy and a seven-day-old baby girl. Historian Elizabeth Oyler suggests that "the elevated poignancy of the death of an heir" probably accounts for the dramatic license taken by the anonymous author of the *Yoshitsune* version (Oyler, p. 188, footnote).

Page 152: "How delightful . . . carried away!": Helen McCullough, *Yoshitsune*, p. 285.

Page 152: "That monk is crazy" and "Stay away . . . he'll do": Ibid., p. 287.

Page 153: "Wait for me . . . branches off" and "Join me in the next world": Ibid., p. 288.

Pages 154–155 "My wife?," "She lies dead by your side," and "Quickly, quickly . . . house": Ibid., p. 292.

Hiraizumi today: Only two buildings remain from Yoshitsune's time, both on the grounds of the Chūsonji Temple. One is the magnificent Hall of Gold, now encased in a concrete structure to protect it from the elements. The nearby museum displays the black lacquered wooden box in which Yasuhira's head was entombed. Inside the temple complex is a special shrine devoted to Benkei. The site of Yoshitsune's suicide on a ridge overlooking the river is marked with a small shrine, and inside is a statue of him in full armor. Every May, Hiraizumi celebrates Yoshitsune with a re-creation of his return to Hiraizumi in 1187; the festival also includes a Benkei Strongman Competition.

EPILOGUE: THE SAMURAI WEEPS

Page 157: Yoshitsune's remains: We don't know what happened to Yoshitsune's body parts. Presumably they were quietly disposed of. Yoritomo wouldn't have wanted any sort of known grave, because that might have encouraged veneration. But he also wouldn't have wanted to display Yoshitsune's head beside the prison gate in Kyoto. Although Yoritomo had proclaimed Yoshitsune a criminal, his half brother was still a high-ranking member of his own family.

Page 157: The examination of Yoshitsune's head: Morris, *Nobility of Failure*, p. 101, and Sato, pp. 155–56.

Pages 157–58: Yoritomo's Hiraizumi campaign: Yiengpruksawan, pp. 161–65; Mass, *Yoritomo*, pp. 137–39; Mass, *Warrior Government*, pp. 145–46; and Friday, *Samurai, Warfare*, pp. 47–48.

Page 158: Yoritomo's punishment of those not joining the campaign: Friday, *Samurai, Warfare*, pp. 47–48.

Page 158: "the treasures of three generations": Yiengpruksawan, p. 161.

Page 158: The Kamakura shrine built to honor Yoshitsune and the Fujiwara: The shrine burned down in the early fifteenth century and was never rebuilt. Collcutt, pp. 115–16.

Pages 158–159: Yoritomo's entry into Kyoto: Brown and Ishida, p. 153.

Page 159: The death of Go-Shirakawa: Ibid., pp. 155–56. The Retired Emperor suffered from "an enlarged abdomen and painful urination," which may have been due to prostate or bladder cancer (Dr. Paul Blumenthal, Stanford University School of Medicine, personal communication, 2013).

Page 159: Yoritomo's appointment as shogun: Morris, *Nobility of Failure*, p. 104. At the time the title was not particularly significant, but it became so later.

Page 159: Yoritomo's death and the ghosts: Blomberg, *Heart of the Warrior*, p. 138.

Page 159: The death of Kagetoki: Brown and Ishida, pp. 179–80.

Page 160: The death of Yoritomo's son Yoriie: See the *Gukanshō* (ibid., p. 179) for a revolting account.

Page 160: Sanetomo's appointment as shogun: Ibid., p. 180.

Page 160: Sanetomo's death: Ibid., pp. 190–91.

Page 160: The political machinations of Yoritomo's widow, Hōjō Masako: See historian Pierre Souyri's analysis of Masako, whom he calls "a kimono-clad Lady Macbeth" (Souyri, *World Turned Upside Down*, pp. 49–52).

Page 161: Yoshitsune's legacy: As historian Helen McCullough has written, Yoshitsune "remains the greatest romantic hero, and probably the single most famous man, in all of premodern Japanese history" (Helen McCullough, *Yoshitsune*, p. 5).

Page 161: Heian aesthetics and martial artistry: As historian Karl Friday notes, "Only in Japan did martial training appropriate the status—as well as the forms, the vocabulary, the teaching methods, and even the ultimate goals—of the fine arts" (Friday, *Legacies of the Sword*, p. 4).

Page 161: Compilation of *The Tale of the Heike*: Helen McCullough, *Genji and Heike*, pp. 251–53, and *Tale of the Heike*, p. 7. Interestingly, though the *Heike* has long been considered a warrior tale, scholar Barbara Ruch believes that Kakuichi, the author of the most famous version of the *Heike*, has threaded the stories of women through the tale "like beads on a rosary" in order to frame the entire epic "with the victorious salvation of women" (Ruch, p. 534).

Page 161: "wrote with . . . Yoshitsune's activities": Yoshida Kenkō, as quoted in Helen McCullough, *Tale of the Heike*, p. 7.

Page 161: Impact of *The Tale of the Heike*: Helen McCullough,

Genji and Heike, pp. 253–54, and Blomberg, *Heart of the Warrior*, p. xi. According to McCullough, "We can probably say that no single Japanese literary work has influenced so many writers in so many genres for so long a time as the *Heike*, and that no era in the Japanese past can today match the romantic appeal of the late twelfth century" (Helen McCullough, *Genji and Heike*, p. 254).

Page 162: The Hokkaido and Genghis Khan legends: Helen McCullough, *Yoshitsune*, p. 61, and Morris, *Nobility of Failure*, p. 101.

Pages 162–63: Yoshitsune's suicide: Historian Mark L. Blum writes: "It is worth noting that *seppuku* was still an unusual way to self-destruct at the time of the events described, and indeed this story of Yoshitsune may have been a catalyst for its later normative status; it is only well after the Genpei War that *seppuku* became de rigueur for any warrior wishing to take his own life" (Blum, p. 152). As historian Maurice Pinguet says (as translated by Rosemary Morris), "In medieval Japan, the cruel, unbending and arrogant rituals of *seppuku* gave suicidal impulses a moral prestige that no other civilization has accorded them" (Pinguet, p. 95).

Page 163: "Paddies and wild . . . stood," "Yoshitsune shut . . . grass," and "A dream . . . grasses": Helen McCullough, *Classical Japanese Prose*, p. 537.

Remaining artifacts from Yoshitsune's time: In addition to the handful of existing buildings dating from the Heian period, there are two sets of red-laced Japanese armor and one set of sleeve armor that date from the late Heian or early Kamakura period and are said to be associated with Yoshitsune. A set of yellow-laced armor is said to be associated with Yoshitsune's uncle Minamoto Tametomo. However, the links to Yoshitsune and Tametomo probably have more to do with eagerness to be associated with famous historical figures rather than the objects' actual historical pedigree. All four objects have been designated National Treasures by the Japanese government.

BIBLIOGRAPHY

Sources marked with an asterisk (*) are English translations of Japanese sources dating from the tenth to fifteenth centuries.

Adolphson, Mikael S. "Benkei's Ancestors: Monastic Warriors in Heian Japan." In *Currents in Medieval Japanese History: Essays in Honor of Jeffrey P. Mass*, edited by Gordon M. Berger, Andrew Edmund Goble, Lorraine F. Harrington, and G. Cameron Hurst III, 87–121. Los Angeles: Figueroa, 2009.

Arnn, Barbara Louise. "Medieval Fiction and History in the *Heike monogatari* Story Tradition." Unpublished PhD thesis, Indiana University, 1984.

Ashkenazi, Michael. *Handbook of Japanese Mythology*. Oxford: Oxford University Press, 2003.

Blomberg, Catharina. *The Heart of the Warrior: Origins and Religious Background of the Samurai System in Feudal Japan*. London: Routledge, 1994.

———. "A Strange White Smile: A Survey of Tooth-Blackening and Other Dental Practices in Japan." *Japan Forum* 2, no. 2 (November 1990): 243–251.

Blum, Mark L. "Collective Suicide at the Funeral of Jitsunyo: Mimesis or Solidarity?" In *Death and the Afterlife in Japanese Buddhism*, edited by Jacqueline I. Stone and Mariko Namba Walter, 137–74. Honolulu: University of Hawai'i Press, 2008.

Bodiford, William M., "The Medieval Period: Eleventh to Sixteenth Centuries." In *Nanzan Guide to Japanese Religions*, edited by Paul L. Swanson and Clark Chilson, 161–81. Honolulu: University of Hawai'i Press, 2006.

Breen, John, and Mark Teeuwen. *A New History of Shinto*. Hoboken, NJ: Wiley-Blackwell, 2009.

*Brown, Delmer M., and Ichirō Ishida, trans. *The Future and the Past: A Translation and Study of the "Gukanshō," an Interpretive History of Japan Written in 1219*. Berkeley: University of California Press, 1979.

*Chalitpatanangune, Marisa. "*Heiji monogatari*: A Study and

Annotated Translation of the Oldest Text." Unpublished PhD thesis, University of California, Berkeley, 1987.

Collcutt, Martin. "Religion in the Early Life of Minamoto Yoritomo and the Early Kamakura Bakufu." In *Religion in Japan: Arrows to Heaven and Earth*, edited by P. F. Kornicki and I. J. McMullen, 90–119. Cambridge: Cambridge University Press, 1996.

Conlan, Thomas D. "Traces of the Past: Documents, Literacy, and Liturgy in Medieval Japan." In *Currents in Medieval Japanese History: Essays in Honor of Jeffrey P. Mass*, edited by Gordon M. Berger, Andrew Edmund Goble, Lorraine F. Harrington, and G. Cameron Hurst III, 19–50. Los Angeles: Figueroa, 2009.

Ellwood, Robert. *Introducing Japanese Religion*. London: Routledge, 2008.

Farris, William Wayne. "Famine, Climate, and Farming in Japan, 670–1100." In *Heian Japan: Centers and Peripheries*, edited by Mikael Adolphson, Edward Kamens, and Stacie Matsumoto, 275–304. Honolulu: University of Hawai'i Press, 2007.

———. *Heavenly Warriors: The Evolution of Japan's Military, 500–1300*. Cambridge, MA: Harvard University Press, 1992.

———. *Japan's Medieval Population: Famine, Fertility, and Warfare in a Transformative Age*. Honolulu: University of Hawai'i Press, 2006.

———. *Japan to 1600: A Social and Economic History*. Honolulu: University of Hawai'i Press, 2009.

———. "Shipbuilding and Nautical Technology in Japanese Maritime History: Origins to 1600." *The Mariner's Mirror* 95, no. 3 (August 2009): 260–83.

Friday, Karl. "The Dawn of the Samurai." In *Japan Emerging: Premodern History to 1850*, edited by Karl Friday, 178–188. Boulder, CO: Westview, 2012.

———. *The First Samurai: The Life and Legend of the Warrior Rebel Taira Masakado*. Hoboken, NJ: John Wiley and Sons, 2007.

———. *Hired Swords: The Rise of Private Warrior Power in Early Japan*. Stanford, CA: Stanford University Press, 1992.

———. *Legacies of the Sword: The Kashima-Shinryū and Samurai Martial Culture*. With Fumitake Seki. Honolulu: University of Hawai'i Press, 1997.

———. "Lordship Interdicted: Taira no Tadatsune and the Limited Horizons of Warrior Ambition." In *Heian Japan: Centers and Peripheries*, edited by Mikael Adolphson, Edward Kamens, and Stacie Matsumoto, 329–356. Honolulu: University of Hawai'i Press, 2007.

———. "Might Makes Right: Just War and Just Warfare in Early Medieval Japan." In *The Ethics of War in Asian Civilizations: A Comparative Perspective*, edited by Torkel Brekke, 159–84. London: Routledge, 2006.

———. *Samurai, Warfare, and the State in Early Medieval Japan*. London: Routledge, 2004.

———. "They Were Soldiers Once: The Early Samurai and the Imperial Court." In *War and State Building in Medieval Japan*, edited by John A. Ferejohn and Frances McCall Rosenbluth, 21–52. Stanford, CA: Stanford University Press, 2010.

———. "Valorous Butchers: The Art of War During the Golden Age of the Samurai." *Japan Forum* 5, no. 1 (1993): 1–19.

———. "What a Difference a Bow Makes: The Rules of War in Early Medieval Japan." In *Currents in Medieval Japanese History: Essays in Honor of Jeffrey P. Mass*, edited by Gordon M. Berger, Andrew Edmund Goble, Lorraine F. Harrington, and G. Cameron Hurst III, 53–86. Los Angeles: Figueroa, 2009.

Fuse, Toyomasa. "Suicide and Culture in Japan: A Study of Seppuku as an Institutionalized Form of Suicide." *Social Psychiatry* 15, no. 2 (1980): 57–63.

Goble, Andrew Edmund. "War and Injury: The Emergence of Wound Medicine in Medieval Japan." *Monumenta Nipponica* 60, no. 3 (2005): 297–338.

Goodwin, Janet R. *Selling Songs and Smiles: The Sex Trade in Heian and Kamakura Japan*. Honolulu: University of Hawai'i Press, 2007.

Hall, John W. "Kyoto as Historical Background." In *Medieval Japan: Essays in Institutional History*, edited by John W. Hall and Jeffrey P. Mass, 3–38. New Haven, CT: Yale University Press, 1974.

Hurst, G. Cameron III. *Armed Martial Arts of Japan: Swordsmanship and Archery*. New Haven, CT: Yale University Press, 1998.

———. "Insei." In *The Cambridge History of Japan*, vol. 2, *Heian Japan*, edited by Donald H. Shively and William H. McCullough: 576–643. Cambridge: Cambridge University Press, 1999.

Irvine, Gregory. *The Japanese Sword: The Soul of the Samurai*. Trumbull, CT: Weatherhill, 2000.

Jameson, E. W., Jr. *The Hawking of Japan: The History and Development of Japanese Falconry*. Davis, CA: Lawton Kennedy, 1962.

*Jones, S. W., trans. *Ages Ago: Thirty-Seven Tales from the Konjaku Monogatari Collection*. Cambridge, MA: Harvard University Press, 1959.

Kasahara, Kazuo, ed. *A History of Japanese Religion*. Tokyo: Kosei, 2001.

Keegan, John. *A History of Warfare*. New York: Knopf, 1993.

———. *The Mask of Command*. New York: Viking, 1987.

*Kim, Yung-Hee. *Songs to Make the Dust Dance: The Ryōjin Hishō of Twelfth-Century Japan*. Berkeley: University of California Press, 1994.

Kitagawa, Joseph M. *On Understanding Japanese Religion*. Princeton, NJ: Princeton University Press, 1987.

Mass, Jeffrey P. "The Emergence of the Kamakura Bakufu." In *Medieval Japan: Essays in Institutional History*, edited by John W. Hall and Jeffrey P. Mass, 127–56. New Haven, CT: Yale University Press, 1974.

———. "The Kamakura Bakufu." In *The Cambridge History of Japan*, vol. 3, *Medieval Japan*, edited by Kōzō Yamamura, 46–88. Cambridge, UK: Cambridge University Press, 1990.

———. *Warrior Government in Early Medieval Japan: A Study of the Kamakura Bakufu, Shugo, and Jitō*. New Haven, CT: Yale University Press, 1974.

———. *Yoritomo and the Founding of the First Bakufu: The Origins of Dual Government in Japan*. Stanford, CA: Stanford University Press, 1999.

McCullough, Helen. "Aristocratic Culture." In *The Cambridge History of Japan*, vol. 2, *Heian Japan*, edited by Donald H. Shively and William H. McCullough, 390–448. Cambridge: Cambridge University Press, 1999.

*———, ed. *Classical Japanese Prose: An Anthology.* Stanford, CA: Stanford University Press, 1990.

*———, trans. *Genji and Heike: Selections from "The Tale of Genji" and "The Tale of the Heike."* Stanford, CA: Stanford University Press, 1994.

*———, trans. *The Tale of the Heike.* Stanford, CA: Stanford University Press, 1988.

*———, trans. *Yoshitsune: A Fifteenth-Century Japanese Chronicle.* Stanford, CA: Stanford University Press, 1966.

McCullough, William Hoyt. "The Capital and Its Society." In *The Cambridge History of Japan*, vol. 2, *Heian Japan*, edited by Donald H. Shively and William H. McCullough, 97–182. Cambridge: Cambridge University Press, 1999.

Meech-Pekarik, Julia. "Death of a Samurai." *Apollo* 121, no. 276 (February 1985): 108–13.

Miller, Jessica A. *Reiki's Birthplace: A Guide to Kurama Mountain.* Sedona, CA: Infinite Light Healing Studies Center, 2006.

Moeshart, Herman J. "Women in the *Heike monogatari*." In *Women in Japanese Literature*, edited by Erika G. de Poorter, 27–38. Leiden, Netherlands: Netherlands Association for Japanese Studies, 1981.

Morris, Ivan. *The Nobility of Failure: Tragic Heroes in the History of Japan.* New York: Farrar, Straus, and Giroux, 1975.

———. *The World of the Shining Prince: Court Life in Ancient Japan.* New York: Kodansha, 1964.

*Murasaki, Shikibu. *The Tale of Genji.* Translated by Edward G. Seidensticker. Tokyo: Tuttle, 1976.

Nagahara, Keiji. "The Medieval Peasant." In *The Cambridge History of Japan*, vol. 3, *Medieval Japan*, edited by Kōzō Yamamura, 301–43. Cambridge: Cambridge University Press, 1990.

Oyler, Elizabeth. *Swords, Oaths and Prophetic Visions: Authoring Warrior Rule in Medieval Japan.* Honolulu: University of Hawai'i Press, 2006.

Pinguet, Maurice. *Voluntary Death in Japan.* Translated by Rosemary Morris. Cambridge, UK: Polity, 1993.

*Reischauer, Edwin O., and Joseph K. Yamagiwa, trans. *Translations from Early Japanese Literature.* Cambridge, MA: Harvard University Press, 1972.

Robinson, H. Russell. *Oriental Armour*. Mineola, NY: Dover Publications, 2002. Originally published 1967 by Walker and Company, New York.

Ruch, Barbara. "The Other Side of Culture in Medieval Japan." In *The Cambridge History of Japan*, vol. 3, *Medieval Japan*, edited by Kōzō Yamamura, 500–543. Cambridge: Cambridge University Press, 1990.

Sakai, Toshinobu, and Alexander Bennett. *A Bilingual Guide to the History of Kendo*. Tokyo: Tankobon, 2010.

Sato, Hiroaki. *Legends of the Samurai*. 1st paperback ed. New York: Overlook Duckworth, 2012.

Segal, Ethan. *Coins, Trade, and the State: Economic Growth in Early Medieval Japan*. Cambridge, MA: Harvard University Asia Center, Harvard University Press, 2011.

———. "The *Shoen* System." In *Japan Emerging: Premodern History to 1850*, edited by Karl F. Friday, 167–177. Boulder, CO: Westview, 2012.

Seward, Jack. *Hara-Kiri: Japanese Ritual Suicide*. Rutland, VT: Tuttle, 1968.

*Shinoda, Minoru, trans. *The Founding of the Kamakura Shogunate 1180–1185: With Selected Translations from the "Azuma kagami."* New York: Columbia University Press, 1960.

Smith, Whitney. *Flags Through the Ages and Across the World*. New York: McGraw-Hill, 1975.

Sollier, Andre, and Zsolt Gyorbiro. *Japanese Archery: Zen in Action*. New York: Walker/Weatherhill, 1969.

Souyri, Pierre Francois. "Autonomy and War in the Sixteenth-Century Iga Region and the Birth of the Ninja Phenomenon." In *War and State Building in Medieval Japan*, edited by John A. Ferejohn and Frances McCall Rosenbluth, 110–23. Stanford, CA: Stanford University Press, 2010.

———. *The World Turned Upside Down: Medieval Japanese Society*. New York: Columbia University Press, 2001.

Takeuchi, Risō. "The Rise of the Warriors." In *The Cambridge History of Japan*, vol. 2., *Heian Japan*, edited by Donald H. Shively and William H. McCullough, 644–710. Cambridge: Cambridge University Press, 1999.

*Tyler, Royall, trans. *Before "Heike" and After:* Hōgen, Heiji,

Jōkyūki. Charleston, SC: CreateSpace Independent Publishing Platform, 2012.

*———, trans. *The Tale of the Heike*. New York: Viking, 2012.

*Ury, Marian, trans. *Tales of Times Now Past: Sixty-Two Stories from a Medieval Japanese Collection*. Berkeley: University of California Press, 1979.

Varley, Paul. "Cultural Life in Medieval Japan." In *The Cambridge History of Japan*, vol. 3, *Medieval Japan*, edited by Kōzō Yamamura, 447–499. Cambridge: Cambridge University Press, 1990.

———. *Warriors of Japan: As Portrayed in the War Tales*. Honolulu: University of Hawai'i Press, 1994.

Vollmer, Klaus. "Buddhism and the Killing of Animals in Premodern Japan." In *Buddhism and Violence*, edited by Michael Zimmerman, 195–212. Lumbini, Nepal: Lumbini International Research Institute, 2006.

Von Verschuer, Charlotte. "Life of Commoners in the Provinces: The *Owari no gebumi* of 988." In *Heian Japan: Centers and Peripheries*, edited by Mikael Adolphson, Edward Kamens, and Stacie Matsumoto, 305–28. Honolulu: University of Hawai'i Press, 2007.

*Wilson, William R., trans. *Hōgen monogatari: Tale of the Disorder in Hōgen*. Ithaca, NY: East Asia Program, Cornell University, 2001.

———. "The Way of the Bow and Arrow: The Japanese Warrior in *Konjaku monogatari*." *Monumenta Nipponica* 28, no. 2 (summer 1973): 177–90.

Yiengpruksawan, Mimi Hall. *Hiraizumi: Buddhist Art and Regional Politics in Twelfth-Century Japan*. Cambridge, MA: Harvard University Press, 1998.

AND IF YOU'RE STILL NOT SATISFIED:

For videos, images, and other interesting tidbits related to Yoshitsune, his times, and how his story has been told through the centuries, please visit the author's website at **www.pamelasturner.com**.

INDEX

233